UNUSUAL BIBLE
INTERPRETATIONS

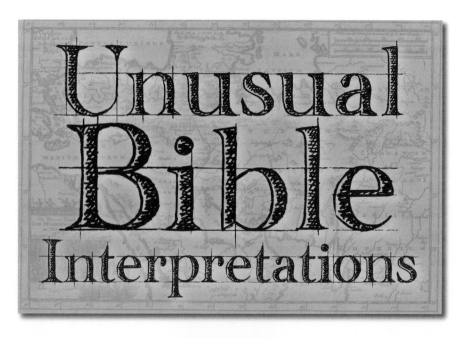

HOSEA

Israel Drazin

gefen גפן
publishing house בית הוצאה לאור
JERUSALEM ◆ NEW YORK   Est. 1981

Cover design: Leah Ben Avraham/ Noonim Graphics
Typesetting: Orgad Studio

ISBN: 978-965-229-888-1

1 3 5 7 9 8 6 4 2

Gefen Publishing House Ltd.
6 Hatzvi Street
Jerusalem 94386, Israel
972-2-538-0247
orders@gefenpublishing.com

Gefen Books
11 Edison Place
Springfield, NJ 07081
516-593-1234
orders@gefenpublishing.com

www.gefenpublishing.com

Printed in Israel

Library of Congress Cataloging-in-Publication Data

Names: Drazin, Israel, 1935- author.
Title: Unusual Bible interpretations : Hosea / by Israel Drazin.
Description: Springfield, NJ ; Jerusalem : Gefen Publishing House, [2016] |
  Includes bibliographical references and index.
Identifiers: LCCN 2016024458 | ISBN 9789652298881
Subjects: LCSH: Bible. Hosea--Criticism, interpretation, etc.
Classification: LCC BS1565.52 .D73 2016 | DDC 224/.606--dc23
LC record available at https://lccn.loc.gov/2016024458

Dedicated to Dina

~ ~ Thirty-five books by Israel Drazin ~ ~

MAIMONIDES AND RATIONAL SERIES

Mysteries of Judaism

Maimonides: Reason Above All

Maimonides and the Biblical Prophets

Maimonides: The Extraordinary Mind

A Rational Approach to Judaism and Torah Commentary

How the Rabbis and Others Changed Judaism (to be published in 2017)

Nachmanides: An Unusual Thinker (to be published in 2017)

Who Was the Prophet Samuel? (to be published in 2017)

UNUSUAL BIBLE INTERPRETATIONS SERIES

Five Books of Moses

Joshua

Judges

Ruth, Esther, and Judith

Jonah and Amos

Hosea

SCHOLARLY TARGUM BOOKS

Targumic Studies

Targum Onkelos to Exodus

Targum Onkelos to Leviticus

Targum Onkelos to Numbers

Targum Onkelos to Deuteronomy

Contents

Acknowledgments

I want to thank Darlene Jospe, who has been performing the first editing of all my books since I began to write *Onkelos on the Torah* with Stanley Wagner. She also helped mightily with formatting and preparing indexes.

I also give thanks to Tziporah Levine, my excellent editor, and to Gefen Publishing House, which has published more than a dozen of my books.

Special thanks, of course, goes to my wife who assists and advises me in many ways, and who is more than patient when I spend so much time writing books.

Introduction

The book of Hosea is filled with interesting information concerning the history of Israel. It tells us what one of Israel's great prophets thought of his people. This introduction provides information regarding the context of Hosea's prophecy. It also offers different ways of understanding God's command to Hosea to marry a harlot.

THE DIVISION OF HOSEA

The book of Hosea comprises fourteen rather short chapters, only one of which is more than 20 verses long, for a total of 197 verses. Hosea is divided into two parts. Part 1, chapters 1–3, discusses events in Hosea's life. Part 2, chapters 4–14, makes up the remainder of the book, in which Hosea berates the people of the northern nation of Israel for their bad behavior.

THE REIGN OF JEROBOAM II

The book of Hosea depicts life during the prosperous reign of Jeroboam II in the northern kingdom of Israel, where Hosea lived and prophesied. Jeroboam reigned for forty-one years in the mid-eighth century BCE, just before the northern nation was destroyed by the Assyrians in 722 BCE. While it is difficult to determine the exact years of Jeroboam's rule, it was approximately from 782 to 743 BCE.[1] He was the fourteenth king of the northern nation of Israel.

---

1. Some date Jeroboam's kingship from 790 to 749, and other scholars offer other dates, For example, the *Encyclopaedia Judaica* (vol. 8, "Hosea" [Keter, 1971–1972]) has the dates 784–746. The difficulty in assigning precise dates is that the Bible is not clear on dates.

The Israelites acted improperly and at least four prophets criticized the nation – Hosea, Amos,[2] Micah, and First Isaiah – focusing on what they considered wrong. Jonah in II Kings 14 also spoke in God's name, but he took a positive approach, prophesying that Jeroboam II should expand his kingdom.[3] The prosperous reign of Jeroboam II was followed by a marked decline and assassinations, which many scholars see Hosea referring to in this book.

DID HOSEA RESTRICT HIS PROPHECY TO THE NORTHERN KINGDOM?

Many scholars are bothered by the book's introduction (Hosea 1:1). It begins by listing four kings of Judah and ends by mentioning only Jeroboam II of Israel. Why are the kings of Judah mentioned? Secondly, according to the *Encyclopaedia Judaica* two of the Judean kings reigned after Jeroboam's death: it dates Jeroboam II's death at 746 BCE, before the reign of Ahaz (733 – 727 BCE) and Hezekiah (727 – 698 BCE). Why is only Jeroboam II's reign mentioned in verse 1 and not the six kings who ruled in Israel after Jeroboam II, during the reign of the Judean kings? Thirdly, why are very short critiques of Judah dispersed in this book if it is devoted to a prophet speaking to his nation Israel?

Many scholars claim that after Hosea's death and after the destruction of Israel, his book made its way south to Judah along with many Israelites who had escaped the Assyrian onslaught, and Judeans took the book and altered it with what they felt was proper. The scholars add that it is possible that the first passage was one of their enhancements and it is likely that they did not have a clear understanding of the chronology of the two kingdoms and did not know the names of all the Israelite kings, or only mentioned Jeroboam II because they felt that Hosea's primary mission was carried out during his kingship.[4]

THE NATURE OF THE PEOPLE'S TRANSGRESSION

Hosea states repeatedly that the people abandoned God and should return. He

---

2. Amos, for example, scolded the Israelites for the mistreatment of the poor. In this volume I will focus on what bothered Hosea.

3. Scholars debate whether the Jonah of II Kings is the same person as in the biblical book Jonah. There is also debate regarding who came first, Amos or Hosea. Surprisingly, none of the four prophets who lived and prophesied at the same time mentions the others.

4. See, for example, the Interpreter's Bible (George A. Buttrick, ed., vol. 6, *Lamentations, Ezekiel, Daniel, Twelve Prophets* [New York: Abingdon, 1957]) and the *Encyclopaedia Judaica*.

compared the Israelite abandonment to his wife who left him and committed adultery, but he does not explicitly say that they worshipped idols. Most commentators, such as Abarbanel, nevertheless contend that the prophet is criticizing the Israelites – the kings, priests, false prophets, and people – for worshipping idols, and foretelling that they will be punished by having their land destroyed and the people driven into exile. While this claim may be true, the prophet's explicit criticism focuses only on the people's mistreatment of their fellows.

Scholars and rabbis who contend that Israel worshipped idols recognize that while the Five Books of Moses repeatedly warns the Israelites not to serve false gods, the Israelites did not remove all Canaanites from Canaan and many Israelites assimilated and began to revere and depend upon pagan idols either as their sole deity or together with God. This understanding is supported by many stories in the biblical book Judges.

The principle deity of the Canaanites was Baal, a word that means "Lord." The Canaanites understood that Baal was a fertility god. Part of the worship of Baal involved sacred prostitutes, who were kept on the temple staff. Men would engage in sex with these prostitutes as an act of worship. The Canaanites felt that these sexual acts were holy, not degrading. It was seen as a kind of sympathetic magic. Just as the men performed acts that could produce fertility, so too Baal would be induced to reproduce Canaan.

HOSEA'S MARRIAGE

It is only in Hosea that a prophet is commanded by God to marry a harlot (see chapter 1). There are at least four ways of understanding this divine command:

(1) The text can be understood literally. God is imminent, meaning that God is ever present and involved in this world. God commanded Hosea find a prostitute and marry her, for this act would be discussed by the people and afford Hosea an opportunity to dramatically educate the people. This is the view of the Babylonian Talmud (*Pesachim* 87a), Rashi, Kara, Abarbanel, and others.

(2) God is not imminent, but transcendental, meaning that God is not involved in this world. This is the opinion of Abraham ibn Ezra, Maimonides, Kaufmann, and others. In his *Guide of the Perplexed* 2:32–48, Maimonides states that prophecy is not a miraculous conversation between God and a human,

but a natural phenomenon: any very intelligent person of any religion with imaginative skill to communicate what he or she sees and understands can be a prophet. Thus, what the book of Hosea is saying is that Hosea had an insight about what he thought God wanted.

(3) Hosea may have felt the need to marry a harlot, but this is unlikely. It is more likely that he married a respectable woman who went astray after bearing one child. Hosea saw this as an allegory of what Israel had done: at first, the Israelites were faithful to God, but later they strayed and became like a harlot. Despite her act, Hosea still loved his wife; if she abandoned her adultery, he (like God with the nation of Israel) would take her back.

(4) The incident never happened. This is only an allegory that Hosea preached (Radak and Targum).

While we don't know which of these four options is correct, Hosea's message is clear: Since the people abandoned God, just as Hosea's wife abandoned him, Hosea tells the people of Israel that their country will be destroyed and the inhabitants driven into exile. But, he adds, if they return to God, God will save them – for God loves Israel, just as Hosea loves his adulterous wife.

OBSCURE IMAGERY

Much of Hosea's words, particularly the imagery, metaphors, and cryptic allusions, are obscure, and commentators frequently offer opposing interpretations of what the prophet is saying. In addition, it appears that not all of Hosea's prophecies are presented in this book in chronological order.

While the rabbis, other clergy, and scholars repeatedly point out the obscurities in this book, we should not think that this book has no value, or is subject only to confusion. The opposite is true. All good literature is filled with thought-provoking ambiguities and obscurities. There is much to learn in Hosea.

THE BOOK OF HOSEA: PART ONE

CHAPTERS 1–3

Chapter 1

Chapter 1 contains four parts. In part 1 (verses 1–3), God commands Hosea to marry a woman who will abandon him and become an adulteress. Rashi states that God actually instructed Hosea to marry an adulterous woman because it was a necessary emergency measure to impress upon the people that they had behaved like an adulterous woman when they abandoned God and worshipped idols. Radak, on the other hand, felt this was only a vision, an allegory that taught this message. This book does not describe the wife's behavior or Hosea's reaction to it.[1] Part 2 (verse 4) contains a prophecy concerning the punishment to the house of King Jehu, an ancestor of Jeroboam II. Part 3 (verses 5–8) relates the punishment that will be inflicted upon the nation of Israel, namely, that God will no longer show the nation love (the term rachum *can also be translated as "pity"). This will occur after the house of Jehu is punished. The nation of Judah, however, will continue to be loved (pitied). Part 4 (verse 9) underscores that just like Hosea's wife abandoned her husband, so too Israel abandoned God. The opening three chapters of the book speak about Hosea's wife and God's relationship with the nation of Israel in such a way that it is frequently difficult to determine which is being referred to.[2]*

---

1. While, according to Rashi, this event is biographical, the book of Hosea only tells readers about Hosea's marriage. Much of what we would like to know about Hosea – who he was, his history, antecedents, and occupation, etc. – is left unsaid.
2. Yehuda Kil, *Trei Asar*, vol. 1, Daat Mikra (Jerusalem: Mossad Harav Kook, 1973).

1. **The word of the Lord that came to Hosea son of Beeri in the days of Uzziah, Jotham, Ahaz, and Hezekiah, kings of Judah, and in the days of Jeroboam son of Joash, king of Israel.**

    Devar can be translated as "word," as indicated above, or as "matter" (Radak). The Aramaic translation, the Targum, adds that the word was a prophecy.

    The name Hosea means "God saves." It is sometimes written more fully as Yehoshua, which is translated into English as Joshua. The initial Hebrew letter *yud* is sometimes transliterated into English as a J, as in *Yerushalayim* becoming *Jerusalem*.[3]

2. **When the Lord began to speak with Hosea, the Lord said to him, "Go, take a woman of harlotry and children of harlotry, for the land commits great harlotry, being unfaithful to the Lord."**

    The Bible uses the term "take" (*l-k-ch*) instead of "marry" (*n-s-a*) because the ancient way of getting married was for a man to have consensual sex with a woman with the intention of marriage. The word "take" is found to describe marriage in Exodus 2:1 and Deuteronomy 22:13. As indicated in the Babylonian Talmud, *Kiddushin* 2a, the rabbis felt that this manner of marriage was not proper and they therefore changed the way marriages were consummated. The rabbis developed the idea that marriage results when a man gives a woman something of value or a contract that a woman accepts as a sign that they are now married. This later morphed into the practice of giving a ring (something of value), while the contract idea is no longer used, perhaps because it later appeared that marriage was turned into a commercial enterprise. The ancient practice of "taking" (sex) is symbolically remembered in Jewish weddings by the couple standing under a canopy, which symbolizes a room where the couple had sex, and by the couple actually entering a room after the ceremony and staying in it (without sex) for sufficient time to have had sex.

    The phrases "a woman of harlotry" and "children of harlotry" do not necessarily mean that Hosea should take a woman who is already wanton and already has illegitimate children, but a woman who will have children in the

---

3. For the historical context of Hosea's prophecies see the introduction, which provides information on the reign of Jeroboam II and discusses who Hosea's intended audience was – Judah and/or Israel.

future as a result of harlotry (ibn Ezra). Rashi understood that the children of the adulterous wife were not necessarily children of other men, but because the wife had relations with other men, they were suspected as not being Hosea's children.

While Jewish law requires a man to divorce his wife if she commits adultery, Hosea is told not to do so. This symbolizes God's relationship with the Israelites who abandoned God. God should have forsaken them, but was willing to take them back if they would act properly (Olam Hatanakh[4]).

The Targum deletes the story of Hosea taking a woman of harlotry from its translation. It has God telling Hosea: "Go [and speak] a prophecy against the inhabitants of the idolatrous city, who continue to sin. For the inhabitants of the land surely go astray from the worship of the Lord."[5]

3. **So he went and took Gomer, daughter of Diblaim, and she conceived and bore him a son.**

There are several ways to understand who Gomer was: (1) She could have been a respectable woman who only became adulterous after bearing Hosea's son, for verse 3 states that she bore "him," meaning Hosea, a son, while no mention of the child being the offspring of Hosea is mentioned for either of the subsequent two children (Ehrlich).[6] Additionally, the name of the first child is not necessarily negative, while the names of the next two are definitely negative. (2) She could have had adulterous relations with one or more men. (3) She could have been enticed to serve as a pagan temple prostitute who gives her body to worshippers as part of the pagan service (Olam Hatanakh). What is clear and significant to the story is that Hosea loved her, just as God loved Israel despite Israel rejecting God's teachings (McKeating).[7]

Radak, who sees the episode as an allegory, states that the woman was called Gomer based on the root Hebrew g-m-r, "end," indicating that Israel was going to be finished. One opinion in the Babylonian Talmud, *Pesachim*

4. M. T. Segal, *Hoshea*, Olam Hatanakh (Keter, 2002).
5. Translation by Kevin J. Cathcart and Robert P. Gordon, *The Aramaic Bible*, vol. 14, *The Targum of the Minor Prophets* (Michael Glazier, 1989).
6. *Mikra Kipheshuto*, ed. Harry M. Orlinsky (New York: Ktav, 1969).
7. Henry McKeating, *Amos, Hosea, Micah*, Cambridge Bible Commentary (Cambridge University Press, 1971).

87a, sees the name suggesting that many men impregnated her, based on the meaning of the word in the *hitpael* form (*hitgameir*).

4. **Then the Lord said to Hosea: "Call his name Jezreel, because I will soon visit the blood of Jezreel on the house of Jehu, and I will put an end to the kingdom of Israel.**

Jezreel means "God sows." While the text indicated to some commentators that Hosea's first son was given a name with a negative prediction (the Targum understands that it denotes that Israel will be dispersed among other nations), it may be that at first Hosea called his son Jezreel to indicate that all good things come from God; it was only later, after seeing Gomer commit adultery, that he saw an ominous meaning in his son's name.

Jeroboam was a descendant of King Jehu, who gained the throne of Israel after assassinating the reigning king Joram and performing mass murders, described in II Kings 9–10. Hosea, like the prophet Amos in chapter 7, predicts the assassination of Jeroboam's son after he served as king for only six months. The text does not state explicitly what the kings did wrong, and commentators offer several suggestions. While it is true that Jehu followed the command of the prophet Elisha to assassinate the then king of Israel and assume the throne, described in II Kings 10:30, some commentators write that he overreacted. Alternatively, Rashi states that Jehu acted properly in taking the throne, but then he and his descendants served idols.

5. **In that day, I will break Israel's bow in the Valley of Jezreel."**

Israel's bow may be a synecdoche for "Israel's might" or "Israel's army," or it may refer to Jehu, who killed King Joram with a bow in II Kings 9:24. It is impossible to identify the battle in the Valley of Jezreel (Olam Hatanakh).

6. **She conceived again and gave birth to a daughter. Then he [God] said to Hosea, "Call her name Lo-ruhamah [not pitied, or, not loved], for I will no longer show pity [or, love] for the house of Israel, that I should at all forgive them.**

As an illegitimate daughter, Lo-ruhamah may have been unloved. In any event, she serves as a symbol of the nation of Israel, who after abandoning God are no longer pitied. The root *r-ch-m* carries the double meaning of "love" and "pity" throughout chapters 1 and 2.

While the text seems to indicate that this daughter was so named at birth, it is possible that this was either an additional name Hosea gave her or a name he thought about her after some time had passed.

The Hebrew *ki naso esa lahem*, translated here as "that I should at all forgive them," is difficult and has resulted in many different interpretations. The words *naso esa* literally mean "I will surely lift up," which runs counter to the rest of the verse. I translated consistent with the generally accepted translation. However, Ehrlich sees "lift up" as indicating an oath and translates "I swear to you that I will not pity them." Rashi: "I will remember [their misdeeds]." Others see the need to rearrange the letters to *sano esna*, "I will surely hate." Still others: the word "no" (*lo*) earlier in the verse applies here as well: "I will not forgive them."[8]

7. **Yet I will show pity to the house of Judah; and I will save them by the Lord their God. But I will not save them by bow, or by sword, or by battle, or by horses, or by horsemen."**

Verse 7 can be understood as being parenthetical, and verse 8 follows verse 6. While Israel will be destroyed in 722 BCE, Judah will be saved, but not as a result of a battle. II Kings 19:35 recalls that an angel of the Lord destroyed the Assyrian camp when Sennacherib's army invaded Judah during King Hezekiah's reign. Maimonides does not interpret the term "angel" as a heavenly being, but any force that carries out the divine will. This would include rain, storms, and even men and women. Since Judah survived for more than a hundred years after the destruction of Israel, some scholars see verse 7 as an insertion into this book by a scribe many years after Hosea's death, but most scholars disagree and accept the view that this is part of Hosea's prophecy (Olam Hatanakh).

8. **After she had weaned Lo-ruhamah, she conceived and bore a son.**

The weaning period of the time was three years. It is unclear why the chapter mentions that Gomer waited to have a third child until after she had weaned

---

8. Francis I. Andersen and David Noel Freedman, *Hosea*, Anchor Yale Bible Commentaries (New York: Doubleday, 1996).

the second child. Perhaps the verse is suggesting that Gomer was careful for three years; despite continuing her adultery she used some sort of birth control.

9. **Then he [God] said, "Call his name Lo-ammi [not my people], for you are not my people, and I will not be yours.**

The phrase *lo ehyeh lakhem*, translated here as "I will not be yours," is obscure. Ehrlich renders it "I will not be [*ehyeh*] to you," referring to Exodus 3:7, 14, where God reveals to Moses that he is *ehyeh*, and will be with the Israelites and redeem them from Egyptian slavery. The Babylonian Talmud, *Berakhot* 9b, and Rashi and Rashbam in their commentaries to Exodus 3, explain that *ehyeh* signifies "I am with you during your current slavery in Egypt and will be with you in the future." However, Kara understands *ehyeh* in this verse as "will [not] be" and states that the word "God" is implied: "I will not be your God."

Chapter 2

The first three verses of chapter 2 are difficult and perhaps misplaced. Midrash Sifrei[1] states that Hosea 2:1–3 interrupts the chastisements of Hosea chapter 1, and what follows it is the rest of the book of Hosea. Ehrlich and others are convinced that the three verses are not part of Hosea's original prophecy.

Alternatively, an argument can be made that the verses belong with chapter 1 since, despite impending punishments,[2] they foretell a good future for the people and reinterpret the names that are in chapter 1. Chapter divisions were a Christian innovation to aid in identifying places in Scripture, such as being able to say that the Ten Commandments is mentioned in Exodus 20 and Deuteronomy 5. However, the divisions themselves are all-too-frequently questionable. For example, the seventh day of creation should be in Genesis 1, but it was placed in Genesis 2. Similarly, some scholars see 2:1–3 as belonging to chapter 1: The verses clarify that despite God abandoning Israel, God will not abandon them entirely.[3] This is a fitting conclusion to chapter 1 since, as Radak notes, it is customary in Scripture to follow rebuke with consolation.

Repentance is an important theological concept today in many religions, including Judaism. Yet, although Hosea speaks frequently about "returning" to God, he and the other prophets of the time did not mention repentance because the concept did not exist at that time. People today think of repentance as the removal of sin, creating a clean slate, as if the person never committed a wrong. This is not the biblical concept, which sees misdeeds much like a broken egg;

---

1. *Sifrei* Balak.
2. The purpose of the punishments is to prompt Israel to return to God (Olam Hatanakh).
3. This is similar to what is stated in Leviticus 26:44.

once an egg is broken there is no way of pasting it together again. This parallels the biblical concept of vows: once a person utters a vow, according to the Bible it cannot be annulled. Both of these biblical concepts were changed by the rabbis, who allowed annulment of vows and stated that repentance whitewashes misdeeds. See the essay on repentance later in this book.

The first twenty-two verses of this chapter comprise the haphtarah to the biblical portion Bamidbar, which gives the number of Israelites. The numbering of Israel is also mentioned in Hosea 2:1. Both show God's love of Israel.

---

1. **"The number of Israelites will be as the sand of the sea, which cannot be measured nor numbered. And instead of it being said of them 'You are not my people,' it will be said of them 'You are children of the living God.'**

   This promise of the Israelites becoming numerous is found in Genesis 22:17 as an assurance to Abraham. The promise is repeated to Jacob in 32:13, where instead of "sand of the sea," the text is more explicit: "sand of the seashore." Jeremiah 23:22 tells the house of David that it will be as numerous as the "sand of the sea."

   The Targum understands *bimkom* as "the place [where you will be exiled]" and not "instead."

   Deuteronomy 14:1 also calls the Israelites "children of God."

2. **The people of Judah and the people of Israel will come together; they will appoint one leader and will go up out of the land; for the day of Jezreel will be great.**

   This promise is also made in Deuteronomy 30:3.

   In Hosea 3:5, this ruler is identified as a descendant of King David. However, here this person is called "ruler," not king, a possible problem I will discuss in the commentary to 3:5.

   In this verse, Jezreel is reinterpreted as a day when the recombined nation will be replanted with seed. Kil understands "come together" as foretelling that both nations will return out of exile, as Deuteronomy predicts in 30:3. Some commentators see this statement as a difficulty because Hosea could not know that Judah would be exiled in 586 BCE, more than a hundred years after his death. However, Hosea may be predicting the exile, just as he is foretelling the exile of the nation of Israel. Alternatively, he may be saying simply that the nation of Israel will join the nation of Judah, which will still exist at that time.

"Day of Jezreel" is a reinterpretation of how the term was seen in chapter 1. There Israel was to be scattered like flung seeds throughout the exile. Here it refers to the numerous descendants of Israel, as numerous as seeds, who will be replanted in the country of Israel. However, Ehrlich understands that it refers to 1:5, in which God promises to punish the house of Jehu and "break Israel's bow in the Valley of Jezreel."

3. **Say to your brethren 'Ammi' [My people] and to your sister 'Ruhamah' [You are loved].**

The word "say" may be directed at the Judeans, who will welcome the people of Israel returning from exile (Saadiah Gaon and Radak). It may also be meant for Hosea's firstborn: Hosea tells his son to call his siblings henceforth by another name (Olam Hatanakh).

4. **Rebuke your mother, rebuke, for she is not my wife and I am not her husband. She should remove her harlotries from her face and her adulteries between her breasts.**

While the current chapter divisions place this verse in the middle of chapter 2, it should be seen as a new beginning. What follows is an explanation of the prior allegory: Hosea's marriage symbolizes the relationship between the Israelites and God; the Israelites have abandoned the deity in a way I will discuss later in this commentary, and this behavior, like Gomer's adultery, severs the relationship.

The mention of "face" and "breasts" suggest parts of the female body that the woman uses in her seduction, or it could refer to ornaments placed on her head and around her neck, falling between her breasts, used to enhance her looks and entice men.

The term *rebu* used here could denote "rebuke," as translated above, or "take her to court for judgment" (Kil and Olam Hatanakh).

The words "she is not my [God's] wife and I am not her husband" indicate that Hosea divorced his wife. If Hosea's wife married another before she returned to him, then Hosea would be acting contrary to Deuteronomy

24:1–4, which prohibits a man from retaking his wife if he divorced her and she became another man's wife. It is also possible that God is telling Hosea in this parable[4] that God loves Israel to such a degree that God is willing to violate the law in Deuteronomy in order to have Israel love God again. See a similar problem in the commentary to 3:4.

5. **Lest I strip her naked, set her as in the day she was born, make her like a wilderness, set her like a dry land, and kill her with thirst.**

Should we understand that Gomer was punished by being literally disrobed? There is no such punishment mentioned in the Torah. However, Ezekiel 16:35–39 may indicate that such a punishment existed. While the adulterous wife clothes herself to aid in her seductions, she will be stripped of her finery and made unattractive. While her suitors gave her gifts in pay for her favors, she will be left without even water to drink. However, it is more likely that the words should be understood figuratively. Hosea is suggesting that the land, to which Gomer is compared, will be stripped naked (destroyed) and the Israelites who abandoned God will be exiled.

6. **I will not show my love to her children because they are the children of adultery.**

While in verse 4 God speaks to the children, in this verse God states that no love will be shown to the children. The two statements thus seem to be inconsistent. Some commentators argued that verse 4 does not belong to the original text of Hosea and that verses 4–6 should be deleted.

7. **Their mother has been unfaithful and has conceived them in disgrace. She said, 'I will go after my lovers who give me my bread and my water, my wool and my linen, my oil and my drink.'**

A faithful wife depends upon her husband for food and drink, clothing, oil, and wine, but the adulterous wife seeks these goods from her lovers. So, too, Israel no longer depends upon God.

---

4. There are other dramas in the prophets that are most likely parables, such as Jeremiah 27–28 and Isaiah 20.

8. **Therefore I will block her path with thornbushes. I will wall her in so that she cannot find her way.**

    While the Israelites seek aid in the wrong places, God will make it impossible for them to get help from other nations.

9. **She will run after her lovers but not catch them. She will look for them but not find them. Then she will say, 'I will go back to my first husband, for then I was better off than now.'**

    In the future, unlike verse 7, the wife will no longer be able to seduce lovers, even if she runs after them. Hosea is saying that frustrated in their attempt to secure help from other nations, the Israelites begin to realize that they had a better time with God.

    Ehrlich notes that the wife returns to her husband not out of love but because she had a better time with him than with her lovers. Similarly, Hosea describes Israel returning to God for the same practical reason. Ehrlich comments that Hosea was satisfied with Israel returning to God for any reason, even for mundane self-interest, and he adds that apparently Hosea lacked a higher concept of religious service.

10. **She did not know that it was I who gave her grain, wine, and oil, who lavished on her silver and gold – which they used for Baal.**

    This verse mixes the singular "she" and the plural "they." The verse could mean that both the adulterous wife (singular) and the Israelites (plural) give the bounty they obtained from husband and God to lovers and idols. (The term "Baal" here may not denote a particular idol, but idols generally, for there were many idols in Israel that used "Baal," lord, as part of their name.[5]) However, the verse could be speaking about the non-Israelites in the land who give away their bounty to idols, and Hosea is saying that "she," the Israelites, received bounty from God but wasted it like "they," the non-Israelites, do. This later interpretation takes note that nowhere else in Hosea does the prophet explicitly berate Israel for worshipping idols. It also takes into account that "she" in the verse must refer to Israel, so "they" must indicate some other entity.

---

5. See, for example, Numbers 25:3, Joshua 11:17, Judges 9:4, and verse 15 in this chapter (Kil).

The three items mentioned in the verse – corn, wine, and olive oil – are used in Scripture to reflect the land of Israel's fruitfulness, as in Deuteronomy 7:13, 11:14, and elsewhere.

11. Therefore I will take away my grain in its time [when it ripens], and my wine in its season. I will snatch my wool and my flax, [intended] to cover her nakedness.

Since the Israelites misused the bounty, God will assure that they have it no longer. The harvests will fail.

12. So now I will expose her shame before the eyes of her lovers; no one will take her out of my hand.

Now undecorated and without gifts for idols, the wrongful people will be seen for what they are, and no one will aid them.

Rashi, who believed in the notion of *zekhut avot*, "merit of the fathers" – that people can secure aid from God because of the meritorious deeds of their predecessors, as if money was placed in a bank that can be drawn upon by subsequent generations – states that the Israelites will be unable to be saved by this "merit."

13. I will stop all her mirth: her festivals, her new moons, and her Sabbaths, all her appointed festivals.

The new moon was a semiholiday in ancient Israel and was celebrated with a festive meal. While in exile, even if the Israelites want to observe the Sabbath and festivals, the joy of the occasions will be muted.

14. I will ruin her vines and her fig trees, which she said were her pay from her lovers. I will make them a forest, and wild animals will eat them.

Not only will the festivals be muted, even all that the Israelites received during the time they abandoned God will be lost and the land itself will be ravaged by wild beasts, which could denote enemy soldiers.

15. I will punish her for the days she burned incense to the Baals, when she decked herself with earrings and jewelry, and went after her lovers, and forgot me," said the Lord.

While the Israelites dressed themselves lavishly during the time of their abandonment, thinking that they would continue wearing the adornments, they will be stripped of them.

This verse uses the feminine singular "she" in describing the punishment for worshipping idols. It could suggest that Hosea's wife became a temple whore, giving herself to Baal worshippers, or that Gomer's adulterous relations were tantamount to worshipping idols. However, this is not certain. "She" could be understood to apply to the Israelites. This commentary understands "she" to refer to Gomer, as it does in verse 10.

16. **"Therefore, behold, I am now going to allure her; I will lead her into the wilderness and speak tenderly to her.**

While they will be punished severely, Hosea visualizes that the future could be joyful if they return to God.

The mention of "the wilderness" is unclear and could be taken as negative or positive. Numerous explanations have been offered: (1) It may refer to the years in exile, living without God, during which they will realize their mistake (Rashi). (2) It may be that the land of Israel will become as bleak as a wilderness (ibn Ezra). (3) It could refer to a period of meditation about what brought about the catastrophe, similar to the forty-year trek of the Israelites in the wilderness during the days of Moses when they realized their mistake in accepting the negative report of the ten tribes. (4) It may indicate that although Israel is enjoying a time of plenty during the reign of Jeroboam, God will reverse their fortune and the conditions of their lives will be as if they live in a wilderness (Ehrlich). (5) It may describe a honeymoon period in which a couple goes off by themselves to become more closely connected, as in Song of Songs 8:5 (Kil).

17. **I will give her back her vineyards from there, and will make the Valley of Achor as a door of hope. She will respond there as in the days of her youth, as on the day she came up out of the land of Egypt.**

The gifts mentioned in this verse can be seen as wedding gifts from God to the Israelites. Celebratory wine from vineyards will accompany the greeting. The Valley of Achor – meaning "troubling" – was the site of Achan's punishment in Joshua 7, when he acted greedily and ignored Joshua's order; now Hosea says that it will be transformed into a door of hope. The Israelites will be satisfied and enjoy the return to the conditions of the past. They will act as they did when leaving Egypt, which Radak understands as the joyful singing in Exodus 15. Isaiah 65:10 is similar when it states that the Valley of Achor will be turned into "a place for herds to lie down in for my people that have sought me."

18. **In that day," declares the Lord, "you will call me 'ishi' [my husband]; you will no longer call me 'baali' [my lord].**

In contrast to the situation described in verse 4, "for she is not my [God's] wife and I am not her husband," when the Israelites return they will rely only on God. Rashi sees the Hebrew *ishi* as a loving title for "husband," while *baali*, "my lord," denotes negative family relations, with the husband acting authoritatively and mistreating his wife. Ehrlich suggests that Israel will remove itself so far from idols that although they called God *baali*, "my lord," in the past, they will stop doing so and the word *baal* will cease to exist, just as their worship of Baal stopped. Interestingly, while the text states that Israel ceased using the term Baal, "lord," they later used the term Adonai, which bears the same meaning.

19. **For I will remove the names of the Baals from her lips; they will no longer be mentioned by their name.**

This verse is in essence a repeat of the former verse. The word *baal* means "master" and "lord" and was appended to the names of many idols and was even used to describe God, as we use the term "Lord" today. In ancient Israel many Israelites added *baal* to their names, understanding that it referred to the true God. An example is the judge Gideon, who was also called Jerubaal. The Bible mocks people who have names ending with *baal* and substitutes *boshet*, "embarrassment."[6] Hosea is stating that when they return, all associations with Baal will be eradicated.

20. **In that day I will make a covenant for them with the beasts of the field, with the birds of the heaven, with the creeping things of the ground. I will break the bow and the sword and the battle out of the land and make them lie down safely.**

---

6. See, for example, I Chronicles 8:33–34; 9:36, 39–40; 14:7; and II Samuel 2:2, 8, 12, 15; 4:4, 9.

In contrast to verse 14, which states that "wild animals will eat them," in the future there will be total peace; even animals will be tame. This is similar to Leviticus 26:6; Isaiah 2:4, 11:6–9; Micah 4:3; and other places. Similarly, the breaking of war instruments contrasts to 1:7, "I will not save them by bow, or by sword, or by battle, or by horses, or by horsemen." Some read that this promise of peace applies only to Israel, but others see it referring to the entire world (Kil).

One should not imagine that Hosea is describing a messianic age because the concept did not exist during the time of Hosea. Maimonides felt that statements such as Hosea's here and the later similar descriptions of the messianic age should be understood as hyperbole. In the messianic age, he wrote, nature will continue as it is now, but Israel will not be under the control of a foreign government.[7]

21. I will betroth you to me forever; I will betroth you to me in righteousness and justice, in loving-kindness and compassion.

The three-fold statement in verses 21–22 speak metaphorically about the union of God and Israel as well as of Hosea and his wife. The two verses are recited when a Jew dons his *tefillin* so as to remember his close relationship with God.

While the verse mentions betrothal, which in ancient times occurred about a year before marriage, some commentators understand that "betroth" here means marriage (Kil).

In ancient times, the groom gave his bride gifts at the time of marriage; here God is giving the gifts to Israel. One of these gifts is loving-kindness, which contrasts with Lo-ruhamah, "not loved," in 1:6 (Kil).

Ehrlich understands the promises to mean that if Israel is righteous and just, then God will be loving and compassionate.

22. I will betroth you to me firmly, and you will know the Lord.

The term *emuna*, which I translated as "firmly," is used in modern Hebrew to indicate "faith," and therefore many translate the term here as "faithfully." Actually, in biblical Hebrew the term means "firmly" and "steadfastly." The concept of having "faith" does not exist in the Hebrew Bible. It was introduced

---

7. *Mishneh Torah, Hilkhot Melakhim* 11:3.

by Paul in the beginning of the common era, when Paul told non-Jews they could join Judaism. (Early Christianity was composed of Jews who accepted Jesus as God, a prophet, or an important teacher). When Moses lifted his hands during the battle with Amalek with *emuna*, he did not do so with faith, but steadfastly, with firmness.

The phrase "and you will know the Lord" contrasts with verse 10, where Hosea mentions that Israel did not know God. See commentary to 8:14.

23. In that day I will respond," declares the Lord. "I will respond to the heaven, and they will respond to the earth.

Continuing the hyperbolic imagery, Hosea sees a changed nature that sends rain whenever the earth needs moisture.

24. And the earth will respond with corn, wine, and oil, and they will respond to Jezreel.

All the good things taken away during Israel's abandonment of the deity will return in plenty. Jezreel, which was interpreted in 1:5 to connote Israel being exiled, scattered like seed throughout the earth, will now symbolize the bounty of fruits, vegetables, and wine.

Kil emphasizes that this verse should not be understood to imply that God will change the laws of nature. The Babylonian Talmud, *Avoda Zara* 54b, states "the world pursues its natural course"; God does not change the laws of nature.[8] How then should we understand this and similar verses? One possibility is that Hosea is speaking metaphorically, as he does throughout this chapter, and he is essentially saying, "All will be well if you behave." Another possibility is that those who act improperly are also doing acts that harm the world, such as farmers ruining the earth by how they plant, by not giving the ground rest. If the farmers act properly with the earth, it will produce more abundantly.

25. I will plant her for myself in the land; I will show my love to the one I called

---

8. The Talmud gives several examples. One is: "Suppose a man has intercourse with his neighbor's wife; it would be right that she should not conceive, but the world pursues its natural course and as for the fools who act wrongly, they will have to render an account" (Isidore Epstein, ed., *The Babylonian Talmud, Seder Nezikin*, vol. 4 [Soncino, 1935]).

'Not my loved one. I will say to those called 'Not my people,' 'You are my people'; and they will say, 'You are my God.'"

Like the other epithets used in 1:6 and 9 to describe Israel, those mentioned here will no longer apply: repentant Israel will be loved and be recognized as the people of God.

Chapter 3

While chapters 1 and 2 are related in the third person, chapter 3 is narrated in the first person. And while 2:16–25 speaks about the return of Hosea's wanton wife as a metaphor for Israel's return, chapter 3 focuses on the return of "a woman" with a similar character but does not mention Gomer. Therefore, some scholars write that this chapter discusses another woman, perhaps a slave whom Hosea redeems.[1] However, the five verses of chapter 3 can easily be seen as providing the details of how Gomer's return was implemented. This second approach fits nicely with the usual scriptural methodology of first making a general statement and then following up with details. There is also a third possibility, according to which chapter 3 precedes chapter 1: Hosea takes an immoral woman, disciplines her, hopes that she has reformed, marries her, has children, and then discovers that she is unfaithful.

1. **The Lord said to me, "Nevertheless, go, love a woman whom you love though she is an adulteress, as the Lord loves the Israelites though they turn to other gods and love raisin cakes."**

    The Hebrew word *od* may refer to chapter 1, in which case the translation "nevertheless" is proper. Alternatively, *od* refers to what follows and means that God spoke to Hosea "further" or "in addition," in which case chapter 3 speaks about someone other than Gomer. Commentators differ on this point.

---

1. Yehezkel Kaufmann holds this view, quoted in the *Encyclopaedia Judaica*. Abraham ibn Ezra and others believed that the woman of chapter 3 is the same one mentioned in the prior two chapters.

The Hebrew *ahuvat rei'a* (translated here as "whom you love") is rendered by many as "loved by others," but Rashi and the Targum apply it to Hosea, the "woman you [still] love" despite her improper behavior. Hosea feels that God is directing him to resume relations with his straying wife and that God is instructing him how he and she must act during the initial stage of the reunion. The verse states clearly that this tale serves as a symbol of how the Israelites can return to God.

The term *ashishei anavim*, translated above as "raisin cakes," suggests "tempting sweets" or gifts "offered on pagan festivals to Baal in thanksgiving for the harvest."[2] Alternatively, it might be understood as "goblets of wine" (Rashi, Kara, ibn Ezra, Radak, Altschuler, and others). It could also be used as a cure for love sickness, as in Song of Songs 2:5, in which case the verse is saying that Israel's worship of idols led other nations to want alliances with them, and this caused Israel to sicken over its idol worship because Israel did not want this alliance (Ehrlich). Another explanation is that although the plural "they turn to other gods" seems to describe the Israelites as a nation, the plural should be understood as a singular: the wife abandoned Hosea to become a temple prostitute and she did so because she enjoyed sweets such as raisin cakes, which Hosea failed to give her.

Olam Hatanakh raises the questions: Can anyone be ordered to love? Is it proper for God to order Hosea to resume relations with a woman who not only deserted him, but committed adultery? We can answer these questions by saying this is an allegory.

2. **So I bought her to me for fifteen pieces of silver and a *chomer*[3] of barley and a *lethekh* of barley.**

No information is given for why Hosea had to pay money to redeem this woman, nor for why he paid part in money and part in goods. It is possible that he had to pay because she had sold herself to the Baal temple as a slave or perhaps she had sold herself as a concubine to some man and needed to be

2. S. M. Lehrman, "Introduction and Commentary," in *The Twelve Prophets: Hebrew Text, English Translation and Commentary*, ed. Abraham Cohen (Soncino, 1961).
3. "*Homer*, by derivation, means an ass-load" (McKeating). He associated *chomer* with *chamor*, an ass.

redeemed. Ehrlich contends that the money and goods were given by Hosea to his wife. McKeating and others say that this is the bride price that the ancients paid to the girl's father. Rashi, Radak, and Altschuler see the number fifteen as a hint to the date, Nissan 15, when the Israelites were redeemed from slavery, and Radak interprets the mention of barley to show how primitive the Israelites were when they left Egypt, for in ancient times barley was considered the food of the poor people.

Lehrman notes that we have no idea what *lethekh* means; the word is not found elsewhere. He also notes that the biblical price for a slave is thirty shekels of silver;[4] some scholars think that *lethekh* is half of the weight of a *chomer* and some think that a *chomer* and a half is worth fifteen shekels, so the redemption price was the biblical thirty shekels. However, if we recognize that prices change, there is no need to seek a way to show that the woman was redeemed for the ancient biblical price. Additionally, perhaps she was so demeaned that she was only worth half the traditional price.

3. **Then I told her, "You are to live with me many days; you must not be a prostitute or be with any man, and I will be so toward you."**

It is unclear whether Hosea ordered the solitude on his own or at the insistence of God. It is also unclear what Hosea means by "and I will be so toward you." It may mean "you may not be with another man, and I will not come in unto you" (ibn Ezra).

4. **For the Israelites will live many days without king or prince, without sacrifice or [sacred] pillar, without ephod or teraphim.**

While verses 2–3 speak about Hosea's wife, verses 4–5 discuss the Israelites. They, like the wife, need to live alone. But unlike Hosea's wife, who lives alone *after* returning to him, the Israelites must live without the four mentioned religious accessories while they dwell without God in exile. Some commentators associate the first two items with divine worship and the last two with idols; thus, Israel will have to sit bereft for some time of both God and idols.

We no longer know what teraphim were. The matriarch Rachel used them in Genesis 31:19–35. In I Samuel 19:9–17 David had teraphim that seem to have

---

4. Exodus 21:32.

been human size and shape, because his wife placed one or more in a bed to make it look as if David were sleeping there.

Olam Hatanakh notes that sacred pillars were used by the patriarchs,[5] and the reference to them here indicates that in the days of Hosea this manner of worship was not abandoned. This conflicts with Deuteronomy 16:22, which forbids the use of sacred pillars. McKeating states that "no decisive step in laying down firm religious standards seems to have been taken until the end of the seventh century, when Josiah carried through his reform (II Kings 22–23)." See the commentary to 2:4 for a similar problem.

5. **Afterwards the Israelites will return and seek the Lord their God and David their king. They will come trembling to the Lord and to his goodness in the last days.**

Seeking David means seeking a leader from the family of David, a reference to the tradition that the Jews are seeking a resumption of the kingdom led by a descendant of King David. This accords with the prophet Nathan's promise to David that his "throne shall be established forever."[6] "The end of days," as mentioned previously, does not mean the messianic age, but the time when Israel returns to the behavior mandated by God. The concept of return reappears in 5:4, 5:15, 6:1, 7:10, 7:16, 14:2, and other verses, always as a contrast to the abandonment of God.

Based on other verses in the book,[7] McKeating notes that Hosea seems to be against all kingship and regards the institution of the monarchy as a mistake. He suggests that either (1) since it does exist, Hosea will settle for reunion under Davidic rule, or (2) he is opposed to monarchy and visualizes a different form of government, and the words "and David their king" were added by a Judean editor.

---

5. See Genesis 28:18 and 31:13, 51.

6. II Samuel 7:16. As with many biblical statements, this could be understood as hyperbole and mean "for a long time."

7. See Hosea 8:4; 9:9; 10:9–10; and especially 13:10–11.

The Book of Hosea: Part Two

Chapters 4–14

Chapter 4

Hosea criticizes the nation of Israel in this chapter for thirteen behaviors: lack of truth, lack of mercy, no knowledge of God, swearing, lying, murder, stealing, adultery, bloodshed, forgetting the law of God, prostitution, consulting wood objects, and using diviner rods. Several of the offenses are stated in the Decalogue, but the Decalogue itself is not mentioned in the chapter or anywhere in Hosea. More significantly, Hosea does not cite all of the commandments in the Decalogue or speak about violating the Torah of Moses.[1] This and similar omissions raise the question: Did Hosea and his generation know about the Torah?

Ten of the misdeeds in this chapter are social, one refers to forgetting the divine laws, and two focus on superstitious divination. The main focus is on prostitution and adultery, which are mentioned eleven times. Chapters 1–3 use prostitution and adultery as an allegory for Israel's abandonment of God; here Hosea describes some of the ways in which the Israelites abandoned God.

Virtually every verse in chapter 4 is obscure and both rabbis and scholars differ among themselves about what the verses mean and to whom each passage is directed. We might view this chapter as follows: In chapters 1–3, Hosea came to realize that like an adulterous wife, the Israelites have abandoned God. Now, Hosea stands before a group of people either in the temple or a marketplace and criticizes the Israelites for this misconduct toward God, and for the first time gives details. During his harangue, he sees some priests in the group and asserts that they caused the people to neglect the behavior that God desires. Priests were given the task to educate the people but they instead focused on

---

1. The term means "Ten Statements," a Greek translation of the Hebrew name *aseret hadibrot*. It is commonly called the "Ten Commandments," even though it actually contains more than ten.

their personal desires and neglected this duty, which left the people ignorant of the behavior God requires.

We can divide the chapter into three parts: (1) Verses 1–3 is Hosea's charge against his nation; it comprises a list of mostly social misdeeds committed by the people. (2) Verses 4–10 focus on the priests who acted improperly in the temple and neglected their function to educate the people. (3) In verses 11–19, Hosea returns his attention to the people and castigates them for creating an atmosphere of prostitution and adultery, which led them to use articles of divination and abandon God.

1. **Listen to the word of the Lord, Israelites, because the Lord has a charge to bring against you who live in the land: "For there is no truth, no mercy, and no knowledge of God in the land.**

Lehrman suggests that this prophecy of Hosea may have been delivered after the death of Jeroboam II, when three kings succeeded to the throne in one year. This was a time of anarchy, when the bountiful period of the reign of Jeroboam II ended. However, there is no indication in the text regarding when Hosea said this prophecy and there is no real reason to say it was not delivered in the time of Jeroboam during a period of plenty.

The verse begins with *shim'u*, translated above as "listen." The oft-used Hebrew word *shema* is generally translated "hear," which is a passive activity. The Targums universally render it as the positive action "accept," signifying that the listener is required to act.

The rabbis understood *chesed*, translated above as "mercy," to be a good act beyond what is generally required.[2] If understood this way, Hosea would be saying that in all of Israel there is no one who acts beyond basic morality.

The Hebrew *riv* could mean "charge," as translated here and as used in court documents, or "dispute," the way I rendered it in verse 4. Radak suggests that God gave Israel the land of Canaan on condition that the Israelites practice truth and mercy, and they breached the contract.[3]

---

2. This understanding appears in many places in the Babylonian Talmud, such as *Yevamot* 105a.
3. See, for example, Leviticus 18:28, Numbers 35:34, Deuteronomy 30:12–13.

The verse rebukes Israel for not knowing God. Maimonides taught in his *Guide of the Perplexed* that it is impossible for humans to know anything about God. Understanding this, Hosea may mean that the people have no knowledge of the practices God demands of people. The Targum explains that the people have no knowledge of the fear of God, which arguably means the same thing. Smolar and Aberbach explain "fear" in the Targum as "reverence" and "fear of sin."[4] Ehrlich explains: God demands that humans act with truth and mercy. Since there is no truth and mercy in Israel, there is therefore no knowledge of God. The word "know" is also used in the Bible to indicate the sexual act; "to know a woman" implies intimacy. It is therefore possible that another meaning of "knowing God" is to create a close relationship with God by doing what God desires, i.e., acting civilly with others. The phrase "knowledge of God" is found in Isaiah 1:11ff, Jeremiah 7:22f, and Micah 6:6ff. See also commentary to 8:14.

2. **Swearing, lying, murder, stealing, and adultery – they break all bounds, and bloodshed follows bloodshed.**

Ehrlich explains that "swearing" denotes perjury and "stealing" means kidnapping. The Hebrew word *paratzu*, "break out," is unclear, and Lehrman's understanding "break all bounds" is sensible. The Hebrew *v'damim b'damim naga'u*, literally "and blood in blood touches," is also obscure and has led to many interpretations. It most likely means that there have been so many murders in Israel that it seems as if one murder follows another without letup, as Rashi and ibn Ezra explain.

Smolar and Aberbach[5] note that according to the Talmud and Midrash sexual immorality increased in Israel and Judah during the years preceding the destruction of the temple in 586 BCE.[6] Men even exchanged wives.[7] Thus, the Targum and Rashi interpret "adultery, they break all bounds" as "committing adultery, they beget children by the wives of their fellows."

---

4. Leivy Smolar and Moses Aberbach, *Studies in Targum Jonathan to the Prophets* (New York: Ktav, 1983), 156–59.

5. Ibid., 109.

6. *Mishna Sota* 9:9; Babylonian Talmud, *Shabbat* 62b–63a; *Tanchuma Tazria* 11.

7. *Shabbat* 62b.

3. **The land mourns because of this, and all who live in it waste away; the beasts of the field, the birds in the sky, and the fish in the sea are swept away.**

Reading the passage literally, Hosea is stating that the behavior of the inhabitants of Israel toward one another affects the land, as in 2:14 and as in Isaiah 24:4–6; however, the Targum and Rashi understand that "land" means the inhabitants of the land.

Ibn Ezra notes that some see Hosea saying that unlike the flood during the days of Noah when fish were not killed, the evil deeds of the Israelites are so egregious that even fish will die, an interpretation that ibn Ezra calls imaginative "*derash.*" He explains that the land will become so desolate that the scavenging animals will be unable to find food.

4. **But let no one dispute, let no one accuse another, your people are like the disputes of a priest.**

This is another obscure passage and translating it is guesswork. Kil notes that some commentators read the phrase to mean that the Israelites argue with the priests, who are trying to teach them proper behavior. But the Babylonian Talmud[8] interprets the verse as saying: "You Israelites do not act properly, but instead you behave like cantankerous priests who are always quarreling with one another." The rabbis say that the two Judean temples were destroyed in 586 BCE and 70 CE because of *sinat chinam,* the inability of people to relate to others without hatred.

McKeating notes that "Hosea does not suggest that priestly religion is irrelevant or that priests ought to be abolished. He assumes their work to be vital, and his complaint is simply that they do it badly." However, see 6:6, "I desire mercy, not sacrifices, and knowledge of God rather than burnt offerings."

Hosea's message in this chapter is the same as that of Maimonides in his Guide of the Perplexed. In 3:32, Maimonides states that God does not need or want sacrifices, but only "allowed these services to continue" because people influenced by other cultures needed them. In 3:53, he says that God wants *chesed, mishpat,* and *tzedaka* – loving-kindness, true justice, and righteousness. In 3:51, he explains that "those who arrive at the palace,

---

8. *Shabbat* 149b and *Kiddushin* 70b.

but go around it [and do not enter] are those who devote themselves to the study of practical law; they believe traditionally in true principles of faith, and learn the practical worship of God." This is parallel to the priests in this chapter of Hosea, who spend all their efforts on discussing and disputing with one another about these principles and methods of worship, but do not do what God wants.

5. **You will stumble during the day, and the prophet will also stumble with you during the night. And I will destroy your mother.**

"You" most likely refers to the priests, mentioned in verse 4, whose temple functions were performed during the day. The prophets, meaning false prophets, are punished at night because most of their visions occur during their dreams. The phrase "your mother" may be a scribal error, with the original text having been "your people." If so, the phrase would mean that all of Israel will be destroyed, as occurred some few years later in 722 BCE (Ehrlich). However, Hosea uses "mother" in 2:4 to describe Israel.

6. **My people are destroyed from lack of knowledge because you rejected knowledge. I will also reject you as my priests. Because you have forgotten the teaching of your God, I also will forget your children.**

Hosea scolds the priests for causing the forthcoming destruction of Israel. By focusing on temple sacrifices and ritual, they failed to teach the people basic morality. They ignored the teaching of Deuteronomy 33:10, "They shall teach Jacob your laws and your teachings to Israel," and of the prophet Malachi in 2:7, "For the priest's lips further knowledge, and they [the people] should seek the law from his mouth, for he is the messenger of the Lord of hosts."

7. **The more they increased, the more they sinned against me. I will change their dignity into shame.**

The more that the priests increased in number, in wealth, and in power over the people, the more they abandoned their teaching role. As a result, God will turn their glory into shame. This occurred in the year 70 CE when the second temple was destroyed and the priests lost their sacrificial function.

Olam Hatanakh suggests that the ancients changed the text from "they shamed my dignity," so as not to even imply that one can shame God.

8. **They feed on the sins of my people and relish their wickedness.**

Rather than teach the people, the priests seek opportunities to have the people offer more and more sacrifices. They delight when the people act improperly and feel the need to bring sacrifices as a way of removing their misdeed; the more sacrifices, the more food for the priests, since the priests are given parts of the sacrificial foods after they are burned on the altar.

9. **So it will be like people, like priests. I will punish him for his ways and repay them for their deeds.**

Since the people acted improperly because the priests failed to teach them proper behavior, both will be punished (ibn Ezra).

10. **They will eat but not have enough; they will engage in prostitution but not satisfy, because they have deserted the Lord.**

The first phrase, "they will eat but not have enough," refers to the priests who, having accustomed themselves to gluttony, want even more. Having finished critiquing the priests, Hosea turns his attention to the people: the untaught people will engage in prostitution and adultery, but this too will not satisfy. The Hebrew word *yiphratzu*, "break out," is unclear, as the root of the word was unclear in verse 2. It probably means "will not satisfy," and parallels what happens to the priests. Rashi and Kara understand it as "will not have children," but this is unlikely, for why would the Israelites want children from prostitutes.

11. **Prostitution, old wine, and new wine take away their understanding.**

In verses 11–19 Hosea comments on the wrongs the people committed. True, the people were misled by the priests, who focused their and the people's attention on temple ritual instead of proper behavior, but the people themselves were also responsible for not understanding how God wants them to act.

The verse literally states "take away the heart," but the heart among the ancients was the seat of the intellect.

12. **My people consult their wood [idols], and a [diviner's] rod speaks to them, for a spirit of prostitution leads them astray; they are unfaithful to their God.**

Prostitution and intoxication led to the Israelites copying the behavior of the pagans in their midst and, like them, they sought solutions to their problems by using superstitious objects.

13. **They sacrifice on the mountaintops and burn [offerings] on the hills, under oak, poplar, and terebinth, because the shade is pleasant. Therefore, your daughters turn to prostitution and your daughters-in-law to adultery.**

Their reliance on sacrifices, even to God, rather than proper behavior, and their superstitious use of the diviner instruments to seek solutions led family members to become prostitutes, either in the pagan temples as part of the cult or in the streets.

14. **I will not punish your daughters when they commit prostitution, nor your daughters-in-law when they commit adultery, because they [the men] themselves consort with harlots and sacrifice with shrine prostitutes; and a people without understanding will come to ruin!**

The assurances that the daughters and daughters-in-law will not be punished should not be taken literally, although Rashi reads it so. The women will be exiled with the men in 722 BCE. Many of them will be raped and killed. The statement is hyperbolic and should be understood as placing the blame on the men who caused the women to act lewdly. The phrase "sacrifice with shrine prostitutes" does not necessarily mean that the men worship the idols; they may still offer sacrifices to God, but they have sex with pagan temple prostitutes, and when their womenfolk see this, they also engage in prostitution.

15. **Though you, Israel, commit adultery, do not let Judah become guilty. Do not go to Gilgal; do not go up to Beth-aven; and do not swear, 'As the Lord lives.'**

It is unclear to whom Hosea is addressing this warning. Olam Hatanakh states it is addressed to the priests. Rashi states that Hosea is addressing Judah. But it may be part of the prophet's address to the people of Israel, as understood by Abarbanel. Hosea is telling Israel that although they commit many wrongs and even drive their women to do so, they should not seduce the people of the southern kingdom of Judah to act similarly. The Israelites should not prompt the Judeans to travel to the northern temples of Gilgal or Beth-el.

The name Beth-el means "house of God." Because he wants to deride the temple, Hosea calls it Beth-aven, "house of iniquity." If the Judeans did go north to these temples, they should not swear using the name of the Lord because this would be blasphemy.[9]

16. **For the Israelites are stubborn like a stubborn heifer. How then can the Lord feed them like a lamb in a large place?**

In this verse and the verses that follow, Hosea is expressing his (or God's) frustration that there seems to be no way to change the Israelites. They are like a wild beast who escaped, who is running wild in a huge area; shall the Lord catch and feed them as one can feed a tame lamb? Rashi describes the Israelites as a "fattened animal that kicks, so too has Israel waxed fat and kicked."

17. **Ephraim is joined to sorrows; leave him alone!**

Ephraim is another name for the northern nation of Israel because its first king, Jeroboam I, was from this tribe and because Ephraim was the largest tribe in this nation. See the essay on Ephraim later in this book.

The Hebrew *atzabim* could mean "sorrows" or "images" here. If the first, Hosea is saying the nation has no hope; they are doomed. If the second, he is saying they are so entwined in pagan practices that they cannot be saved. JPS translates "Ephraim is joined to idols. Let him alone"; this seems to be incorrect, as discussed in the commentary to 6:6 and 8:4.

18. **When their drinking ends, they take to prostitution; her rulers dearly love shameful ways.**

It is unclear who "their" is: the people or the rulers mentioned at the verse's end. Verse 18 may be a continuation of 17, in which case Hosea may be saying that there is no hope for the people: they are led astray by their leaders' misconduct, and one wrong leads to another. Alternatively, the Targum interprets that the entire verse may focus on the leaders. The first interpretation seems more likely because of the context.

---

9. See Rashi to Deuteronomy 6:13–14, where he states that only people who act as God desires may swear using the divine name.

19. **A wind has bound her up in her skirts, and they will be ashamed because of their sacrifices."**

As a result, the country will be overrun like a sudden violent gust of wind that unexpectedly blows up a person's skirt and shames the person. The Israelites will also be ashamed because of their sacrifices, for they thought that the sacrifices would save them, but they misunderstood what God desires: God wants proper behavior, not sacrifices, as Hosea says in 6:6, "I desire mercy, not sacrifices, and knowledge of God rather than burnt offerings."

Chapter 5

Chapters 5 and 6 can be seen as a single unit, perhaps a long speech that Hosea recited. Like the rest of this book, it is filled with obscurities: we frequently do not know to whom Hosea is speaking, or when and what he is saying. Chapter 5 can be divided into two parts: In 1–7, Hosea critiques the leaders of Israel, including the priests, for distancing the people of Israel from God. In 8–15, he addresses the corruption of the leadership and its consequences (Olam Hatanakh).

In chapter 5, Hosea depicts God's reactions to the misdeeds of Israel, Judah, the priests, and the political leaders. He uses the same terminology found in prior chapters: abandonment, mercy, and knowledge of God. Ten wrongs are listed, four of which were mentioned previously: prostitution, not knowing God, being unfaithful, and giving birth to illegitimate children. Adding the remaining six to the thirteen previously mentioned, we have a nineteen-count indictment. The six new reprimands are a snare at Mizpah and net spread upon Tabor in verse 1, slaughter in 2, pride in 5, Judah moving boundary stones in 10, Israel walking after filth in 11, and Israel turning to Assyria in 13. These are all wrongs committed by the nations of Israel and Judah. Hosea does not mention idols or even allude to worship in the list with the possible exception of "Israel walking after filth," which probably refers to moral wrongs.

1. **"Listen to this, priests! Pay attention, house of Israel! Give ear, royal house! This judgment is against you: You have been a snare at Mizpah, a net spread upon Tabor.**

In chapter 4, Hosea addressed the people and mentioned the priests in only a few sentences; now he addresses the people ("house of Israel"), priests (of the temples of Beth-el and Dan in northern Israel), and the nation's leaders, and criticizes them while foretelling their doom. The term "house of Israel" may refer to the false prophets (Interpreter's Bible) or the leaders of the people (Olam Hatanakh).

I have translated *lakhem hamishpat* as "this judgment is against you." Some commentators, however, translate "it was your duty to administer Judgment," suggesting that the priests and leaders were supposed to teach ("judge") the people, and since they did not do so they themselves will be judged and punished.[1]

Mizpah means "watch."[2] It was a city in Gilead or in the territory of the tribe of Benjamin. It is unclear whether Hosea is referring to this city or he is mentioning Mizpah ("watch") as a sarcastic reference to the fact that the priests and rulers did not watch over the Israelites. Tabor was the area where God helped Barak in his war against Sisera.[3] Rashi, ibn Ezra, Kara, Radak, and others state that Hosea is remonstrating against the nation of Israel for setting guards in these two high places to stop the people of Israel from traveling to the temple in Jerusalem. It is possible that the Israelites were saved in both Mizpah and Tabor and Hosea is rebuking them for choosing these places to abandon God and worship idols.

2. **They that fall away are deep in slaughter, and I am rejected by them all.**

This verse, like others, is obscure. It may refer to the leaders who caused many murders, or the priests whose failure to teach resulted in the people's abandonment of God, and the abandonment was like their death. Although there is no explicit charge against Israel for idol worship in this chapter, the Targum sees it hinted here. Radak read the word "I" in this passage to refer to Hosea, who tries to help the people but is rejected by them.

---

1. Andersen and Freedman, Anchor Yale Bible Commentaries.
2. As in Genesis 31:48–49, Jacob's covenant with Laban: "Laban said, 'This heap is a witness between you and me this day.' Therefore, it was named Gilead. And Mizpah, for he said, 'May the Lord watch between you and me when we are absent one from the other.'"
3. Judges 4:6.

3. **I know all about Ephraim; Israel is not hidden from me. Ephraim, you have now turned to prostitution; Israel is defiled.**

Hosea states that God knows what is happening and although the people may perceive that they are acting piously, God sees their behavior as defiling prostitution. The term "prostitution," used frequently by Hosea, may indicate idol worship, as in Psalms 106:39. Alternatively, it could refer to improper conduct with fellow Israelites or the abandonment of God, as suggested in the next verse.

4. **Their deeds do not allow them to return to their God, for a mindset of prostitution is within them; they do not know the Lord.**

The Hebrew word *ruach*, translated here as "mindset," is usually rendered "spirit." The people's improper deeds have become so ingrained, so habitual, that it is difficult to return them to acceptable behavior. In his essay "*Shemoneh Perakim*," Maimonides warns against the problem of developing ingrained improper habits and suggests that people should instead work to develop habits according to the Golden Mean, moderation, the midpoint between excess and restraint.

While Hosea states that the deeds "do not allow them to return to their God," this is hyperbole, for Hosea actually believes, as we saw in chapter 3, that the people can and will return to God. The Targum renders "they do not know the Lord" as "they have not sought instruction from the Lord."

5. **Israel's pride humbles them; Israel and Ephraim stumble in their iniquity; Judah will also stumble with them.**

"Israel's pride" is unclear. It may denote the rulers of Israel who acted improperly, or the hubris of the people of Israel (repeated in 7:10) whose arrogant self-confidence will be their downfall. The term *v'ana* could mean "humble" or "testifies [against them]."

Hosea may be stating that the same malfeasance exists in Judea, which he will detail in verses 8–15, or he may be recalling the time that the king of Judah joined the king of Israel to fight their joint enemy.[4]

Some commentators consider the repetition of Israel in the verse an error

---

4. I Kings 22 and II Kings 3.

(Interpreter's Bible) or a common doubling as in Numbers 23:23 (Olam Hatanakh).

6. **They go with their flocks and herds to seek the Lord, but they do not find him; he has withdrawn himself from them.**

It is unclear whether Hosea is speaking of Judah, as stated by ibn Ezra and Radak, or of Israel, as the Interpreter's Bible and others contend. When the people discover that their abandonment of God resulted in unfavorable consequences, they think that they can appease God and secure divine aid with sacrifices. But, as stated in 6:6, God does not desire sacrifices; God wants people to act properly with one another.

The Targum renders "he has withdrawn himself from them" as "he will remove his Shekhina from them." The substitution eliminates the anthropomorphic notion that God can withdraw as humans do. The word "Shekhina" is based on the Hebrew word meaning "dwell." While many people, including Saadiah Gaon, understand that the Shekhina is a being created by God to do Godlike activities, this borders on polytheism. A better understanding is that Shekhina is the "feeling that people have" that God is present. Here it would mean that the people will not feel that God is present.

7. **They have been unfaithful to the Lord; they gave birth to alien children. Now a month will devour their portion.**

Returning to the theme of abandonment, the principle theme of Hosea's prophecies, Hosea speaks of children who are *zar*, translated above as "alien." The Targum and Rashi understand it as the progeny of marriages with women of foreign nations. It may also refer to children produced by adultery or prostitution, or the prophet may be saying that despite offering sacrifices, as indicated in the prior verse, the parents have caused their children to also abandon God by following their example of uncivil conduct. Unwilling to describe the people being so removed from God that they are unfaithful to God, the Targum inserts the word *memra*, meaning "word" or "command." This is a typical Targumic addition and occurs hundreds of times in the Targumic versions of Scripture. Here, the people are unfaithful to God's command.

A literal reading of the conclusion of verse 7 is "Now the new moon will devour their portion," which is obscure. We can only speculate as to its meaning. It could suggest that during the festivities of the New Moon, which was a time of joy and feasting in ancient Israel,[5] the people will face a calamity. Or, Hosea may be saying that the country will be destroyed shortly or frequently, month by month, as the Targum has it. Or: this is the month of Av, when the two Judean temples will be destroyed in Jerusalem (Rashi and Kara). Or: the enemy forces will eat the festive New Moon food, not the Israelites (Radak).

8. **Sound the trumpet in Gibeah, the horn in Ramah. Raise the alarm in Beth-aven; [look] behind you, Benjamin.**

The imminent attack implied in the previous verse is coming and the people need to be alerted. Benjamin is in the southern area of the northern nation Israel, and Radak explains that the tribe of Benjamin is warned by the northern tribes who are being conquered that the enemy is at Benjamin's back.

It is unclear whether Beth-aven here refers to a city with this name that is near Beth-el, as Rashi claims,[6] or a derogatory name for Beth-el, as in 4:15 (Olam Hatanakh). See 9:9 and 10:9 regarding Gibeah.

9. **Ephraim will be laid waste on the day of reckoning. Among the tribes of Israel, I reveal what will be.**

The last word of the verse is *ne'emana*, whose root is *a-m-n*. It means "strength" and "steadfastness."[7] Thus the verse could be translated "I will act against Israel with strength." The day of reckoning will occur in 722 BCE, when the events that Hosea foretold will transpire.

10. **Judah's leaders are like those who move boundary stones. I will pour out my wrath on them like a flood of water.**

The offense of the "removal of boundary stones," which is the stealing of land belonging to another, is proscribed in Deuteronomy 19:14 and 27:17. Hosea may be stating that Judah is like Israel in stealing property belonging to another and will, like Israel, be destroyed as quickly as rushing water for their misdeeds. Ehrlich explains that Judah is waiting for its northern neighbor to be over-

---

5. See I Samuel 20.
6. Mentioned in Joshua 7:2 and 18:12.
7. See Exodus 17:12, Numbers 12:7, and more.

thrown so that it can cross into its land and annex it. Ibn Ezra understands the prophet to be saying that Judah is acting against Israel quietly, with stealth.

11. **Ephraim is oppressed, justly crushed, because he willingly walked after filth.**

The Hebrew *tzav*, translated here as "filth," means "command." Numerous interpretations have been offered to explain the phrase: (1) It may refer to Jeroboam I's command to the nation of Israel: Jeroboam formed Israel after breaking away from King David's descendant King Rehoboam. One of his first acts was to establish two new temples in his kingdom so that his people would not travel to the Jerusalem temple in Judah, and he commanded his people to worship in the new temples (Radak). (2) The word *tzav* may be a corrupt form, with the original word being *tzo'a*, "filth" – a disparaging term for "idol." It is rendered in this way in the Septuagint, the Peshitta, and the Babylonian Talmud, *Sanhedrin* 15b and 56b. (3) The Targum does not see Hosea speak about idols here, but states: "their judges have turned to go astray after the money of falsehood." (4) Rashi and Kara explain: Ephraim is following the commands of the Baal priests. (5) It may be the name of a foreign king (Olam Hatanakh).

12. **I am like a moth to Ephraim, like rot to the people of Judah.**

Moths and rottenness eat away clothing; so too will God cause the destruction of the two kingdoms. Both moths and rot act gradually. The Targum has the *memra*, God's "word" or "command," be like a moth and rot, so as to be more respectful to God and not treat the deity anthropomorphically.

13. **When Ephraim saw his sickness, and Judah his wound, then Ephraim turned to Assyria, and [Judah] sent to King Contentious. But he is not able to cure you, not able to heal your wound.**

Rashi understands that the king of Israel was Hoshea, the last of Israel's kings. The Kingdom of Israel existed for 210 years, until 722 BCE. During that time nineteen kings reigned, from ten different families.[8]

Hosea insults the king of Assyria by calling him "Contentious." As a result,

---

8. II Kings 17. The Interpreter's Bible gives the length of Israel's existence as 253 years, and there are other counts.

we have no idea to whom he is referring. G. R. Driver suggests that the letter *yud* in *yarev*, "contentious," belongs in the former word and the reading is "great king."[9] Lehrman, McKeating, and others write that the adjective suggests the folly of King Menahem of Israel, who gave the king of Assyria a hold on his country in 738 BCE.[10] Rashi thinks "Contentious" is Tiglath-pileser III, who was bribed by the Judean king Ahaz to help Rezin, king of Syria, and Pekah, son of Remaliah, in 732 BCE.[11] It is the general practice of Israelite prophets to critique kings for seeking aid from foreign nations. Here, Hosea is saying that foreign kings cannot save the two nations from divine wrath.

Hosea uses the metaphor "heal" here and in 6:1, 7:1, and 14:5.

14. For I will be like a lion to Ephraim, like a young lion to Judah. I, I will tear them to pieces and go away; I will carry them off, with no one to rescue them.

God, or the *memra* in the Targum, will act against Israel and Judah as a strong fierce lion – once it grabs something in its jaws, few people would dare to try and rip it out. The doubling of "I, I" is for emphasis.

15. I will go and return to my place until they acknowledge their guilt and seek my face. In their misery they will earnestly seek me."

Many commentators feel that verse 15 fits better with chapter 6, as an introduction to the three verses in that chapter in which the people think of returning to God (McKeating). The Targum has the Shekhina go to heaven, which could be understood as the people not feeling the presence of God.

---

9. "Studies in the Vocabulary of the Old Testament, VIII," *Journal of Theological Studies* 36 (1935): 295–96.
10. Mentioned in II Kings 15:19f.
11. Discussed in II Kings 16:7ff.

Chapter 6

In three verses – possibly four if 5:15 is included – Hosea describes the people deciding to return to God. They do not reveal what actions they will pursue – whether they will cease worshiping idols, or begin to treat others properly, or something else altogether. Hosea also does not say what prompted the people to "return to the Lord." It is possible that the people of Israel and Judah saw the destruction of the two and a half tribes in Transjordan in c. 732 BCE, and this prompted them to try to return to God. It is likely that they felt that a return to God involved bringing sacrifices, which verse 6 states is wrong or insufficient, as I will discuss. It is clear that neither the Judeans nor the Israelites had a concept of "repentance," for as I explain in the essay on repentance later in this book, the concept did not exist at that time.

1. **"Come, let us return to the Lord. He is tearing [us] but he will heal us; he is injuring us but he will bind up [our wounds].**

    In the following three verses, the people, overcome by the previously mentioned misery, momentarily consider returning to the conduct that God desires. The Targum has the people return to the worship of the Lord, but worship is not mentioned in this book.

    The prophet reuses the metaphor "heal" here as in 5:13, 7:1, and 14:5, as if he considers their behavior a disease.

2. **After two days he will revive us; on the third day he will restore us, that we may live in his presence.**

Scripture uses the notion of three days frequently to indicate a short time, as in Genesis 22:4, Exodus 19:11, Joshua 1:11, I Kings 20:5, and II Kings 20:8. Ibn Ezra states that the number seven in Scripture indicates a complete act, as in the seven days of creation, while the number three – being close to half of seven – implies a shorter period.

Rashi states homiletically that the verse refers to the destruction of the two temples in 586 BCE and 70 CE, but there will be a third temple in the future.

Hosea describes the people as entertaining an incorrect concept of God, according to which God is prepared at any time to receive those who return to him with alacrity, as long as they offer sacrifices.

3. **Let us know, let us press on to know the Lord. As surely as the morning, he will appear; he will come to us like the rain, like the latter rain that waters the earth."**

The people of Israel, or possibly both Israel and Judah, are now in a rush to "know" the Lord – the very concept Hosea repeatedly described the people ignoring. They want to return to the practices that God desires, or the fear of the Lord (Targum). They expect God to rush as they are rushing to remove the calamities that afflict them.

Ibn Ezra appears to understand "know the Lord" philosophically, as knowledge of the universe, as Maimonides does throughout his *Guide of the Perplexed*. Ibn Ezra states: "This is the basic secret concerning all wisdom. This is the human duty. But one cannot 'know God' until the person studies many kinds of wisdom. It is like a ladder that one must climb to reach the highest rung. 'Morning' is mentioned because the wise person who 'wants to know God' must begin by understanding nature, such as the morning. Then little by little the light [of wisdom] will become brighter and brighter [as the light becomes brighter during the day] until the truth is seen." This is good philosophy, but it is doubtful that this is what Hosea had in mind.

"What shall I do with you, Ephraim? What shall I do with you, Judah? Your mercy is like the morning mist, like the dew that disappears.

Hosea sees God noting that the return of the two kingdoms to God is short-lived or, as indicated in verse 6, bereft of human kindness.

4. **Therefore, I cut [them] in pieces with prophets, I killed them with the words of my mouth, and your judgment goes forth like light.**

This verse, like virtually every one in Hosea, is obscure. Hosea may be noting that there were more prophets than he who reprimanded the people and he may be saying that the people did not listen to the prophets and, consequentially, will be killed. However, the phrase *chatzavti ba'neviim* lacks the word "them," and literally means "I have cut [destroyed] with [by *or* among] prophets." If the latter, Hosea may be referring to God killing false prophets, perhaps even Jonah of II Kings 14:25–26 who encouraged Jeroboam to enlarge his kingdom by conquering other lands.[1]

However, it is more likely that the phrase about murdering the people should not be taken literally. It does not mean that God killed them. The people were butchered by the invading army, and the prophets, if this is the sense of the verse, were assassinated by defiant people or the invading army. As a result of their waywardness, God brought this punishment quickly (according to the Targum, as swift as lightning).

It is unclear whether Hosea is addressing Israel or Judah or both in this verse. This is important because it affects our understanding of verse 6.

Andersen and Freedman raise an interesting question here: "One wonders how much he [Hosea] was aware of the ministry of his contemporaries Amos, Micah, and Isaiah."[2] The two scholars recognize that Hosea is following the tradition of the other prophets, but why doesn't he mention them, or Jonah? This question is similar in some respects to the more basic question: Why doesn't Hosea mention Moses's Torah? The failure to obey it would have been a much stronger denunciation than all his other rebukes.

5. **For I desire mercy, not sacrifice, and knowledge of God rather than burnt offerings.**

Andersen and Freedman note that "this verse makes a basic statement which is the foundation of all that precedes" and add that verse 7 "begins a new

---

1. As mentioned above, the Jonah of II Kings may be different than the Jonah of the biblical book by that name.
2. Anchor Yale Bible Commentaries.

discourse." It is therefore lamentable that this verse is as obscure as much of Hosea's discourse.

It is striking and very significant that Hosea is berating the people for offering sacrifices while they neglect mercy and knowledge of God. This denunciation is repeated by Hosea in 8:13 – "They offer sacrifices of fire to me, they sacrifice and eat the meat, the Lord is not pleased with them" – and by other prophets. The basic question is: Did Hosea, a prophet living in the northern kingdom of Israel, consider the worship in the temples of Beth-el, Dan, and elsewhere in Israel to be idol worship? Arguably, there is no verse in the volume that explicitly says so, although there are many verses that seem to imply it and most commentators understand that Hosea is berating his people for idol worship. For example, in 4:15 and 5:8 he calls the city of Beth-el, where an Israelite temple stood, a "house of iniquity." Many commentators understand that he is referring to the iniquity of idol worship.

Yet, since he is not explicit about idol worship, but is explicit about the people's failure to adhere to basic civil norms, isn't it more likely that he calls the temple cities "places of iniquity" because they fail to teach proper conduct?[3] Additionally, if the prophet is scolding his nation in verse 6 for idol worship, why doesn't he say so?

Thus it appears that Hosea is either addressing Israel, and considers their sacrifices to be offerings to the true God, or haranguing the people for thinking that offerings is what God wants when in fact God wants the people to act properly. Alternatively, the prophet is addressing Judah here, and not Israel. He considers Judean sacrifices as being directed to God, but reprimands the Judeans for thinking that this is what God desires. This is the opinion of Abarbanel, and it is consistent with verse 4, which mentions both nations.[4] But the verse is unclear, and Radak claims it is speaking of both kingdoms, and that

---

3. See the discussion in the afterword for a list of other verses that seem to imply that Hosea is speaking about idol worship.
4. Abarbanel also contends that only "mercy" and "knowledge of God" are mentioned because the first refers to all interactions between people and the second to interactions between man and God. This is uncertain since the phrase "knowledge of God" could be interpreted throughout this book as interpersonal conduct that God desires. The phrase here may mean "mercy and all other moral behaviors."

while each generally offered sacrifices to idols, Hosea was addressing the short period when they ceased doing so and sacrificed to God.

Most commentators, Jewish and non-Jewish, are convinced that God wants sacrifices but only when they are accompanied by proper behavior.[5] In the *Guide of the Perplexed* 3:32, Maimonides disagreed. God only "allowed these kinds of service to continue" because the people, accustomed to offering them and seeing other nations doing so, needed to do so as well. He states that the prophets also said that God does not want or need sacrifices. He cites I Samuel 15:22, Isaiah 1:11, and Jeremiah 7:22–23. He could have added Hosea 6:6, 8:13; Amos 5:21–24; Isaiah 14–15; and Micah 6:6, 8.

McKeating translated the verse as "loyalty is my desire, not sacrifice, not whole-offerings but the knowledge of God." He admits that the verse is ambiguous: rather than rejecting sacrifices altogether, it may be emphasizing the issue of priority –"only that loyalty is more important to him [God]." This is also the view of Andersen and Freedman. Lehrman contends that God is not rejecting sacrifices but the "sacrificial act without moral living is rejected by God." And he adds: "Note Hosea's repeated stress upon knowledge of God."

6. **But they are like men who have broken the covenant; they have abandoned me there.**

The word for "men" is *adam,* which led some commentators such as Rashi, Altschuler, and others to understand that Hosea is saying that the Israelites are like the biblical Adam who disobeyed God and ate the forbidden fruit. This interpretation fits in with the word "like." Radak understands that Hosea is speaking about the average Israelite who does not behave appropriately with his fellow. Others render the verse "At Admah they have broken my covenant," referring to Hosea 11:8; Admah was apparently a place that had been recently destroyed (McKeating).[6] Still others see an allusion to the city of Adam, men-

---

5. Altschuler, Kil, and Olam Hatanakh are among those who are convinced that Hosea is not saying that God does not want sacrifices; he is only saying that sacrifices without mercy to others is not acceptable. Rashi and Kara are unclear.

6. Admah was a place that cannot be identified for certain, but may refer to the city mentioned in Deuteronomy 29:22, one of the cities in the plain in the overthrow of Sodom and Gomorrah (Lehrman to 11:8).

tioned and identified in Joshua 3:16. The Targum has "the former generations" being false to God's *memra*.

By "there," Hosea is referring to the cities mentioned in the next verses: Gilead and Shechem. Alternatively, if the reading is Admah or Adam, "there" is one of these cities.

7. **Gilead is a city of evildoers, stained with footprints of blood.**

Gilead was the inheritance of the two and a half tribes – Reuben, Gad, and the half tribe of Manasseh; it was destroyed in c. 732 BCE by the Assyrians. Hosea is telling the people of Israel that unless they come back to God, they will suffer the same calamity and exile that the two and a half tribes suffered.

8. **As marauders lie in ambush for a victim, so do bands of priests; they murder on the road to Shechem, carrying out their wicked behavior.**

Shechem was established as a city of refuge for people who committed unintentional murder.[7] Hosea describes its current status hyperbolically as a place where intentional murderers, even priests, wait in ambush. The overstatement about priests murdering may refer to their failure to teach people proper behavior or that they, like the Israelites, engaged in dishonest and offensive acts.

It should be noted that Hosea uses the word *zima*, translated here as "wicked behavior." It is associated with incest and idolatry, but also with wickedness. In context, because the verse is speaking about acts committed "on the road to Shechem," it is reasonable to translate it as "wicked" here since it is unlikely that the priests were involved with idolatry on the highway. This adds some support to the view that incest and adultery in other Hosea verses should be understood as metaphors for "wickedness."[8]

9. **I have seen a horrible thing in Israel: there Ephraim is given to prostitution, Israel is defiled.**

Hosea repeats his prior rebuke by using the word *sha'aruriya*, translated here as "horrible thing." With the root of *se'ar*, meaning "hair," the word may be used to imply that the prostitution is so egregious that it makes one's hair stand up

---

7. Joshua 20:7.

8. However, "murder on the road" may be a metaphor for destroying the people by teaching them idol worship or by failing to instruct them about moral conduct.

in shock (Lehrman). While the Hebrew does not mention idols, the Targum states that Ephraim is worshipping idols.[9]

10. Also for you, Judah, a harvest is appointed. When I would restore my captive people,

It appears that the predicted "harvest" for Judah will be calamitous, as is foretold for Israel. They will be uprooted from their land as a harvest is pulled out of the earth.

Many scholars, including Lehrman and Kil, are convinced that the second part of verse 11 belongs as an introduction to chapter 7. It should be understood as follows: When the time came when God could reverse Israel's misfortune – God, as indicated in chapter 7, saw that the people had not yet returned to the desired worship. The Revised Standard Version translation of the Bible captured this idea by inserting a space before "When I would restore my captive people," and ending the statement with a comma, to indicate the translators' belief that this part of the verse belongs in chapter 7.

9. According to the Targum, "prostitution" represents the people's abandonment of God in favor of idol worship.

Chapter 7

Moving from the nineteen indictments of Israel and Judah, most of which only apply to Israel, Hosea describes what appears to be the last days of the nation of Israel. After Jeroboam II's long and bountiful reign, Israel endured twenty-five years of political upheaval, during which time six kings ascended the throne of Israel, four of whom were assassinated. The nation and its population deteriorated, and its rulers sought support from foreign nations.

Hosea predicts that the land will be destroyed. He describes the scene of the decline of law and order with bright, beautiful metaphors. He begins and ends the chapter by depicting God lamenting the Israelites' behavior. Kil sees chapters 7 and 8 as a unit containing Hosea's harsh chastisement of his people and the imminent, shattering punishment that will ensue.

1. **When I would heal Israel, the iniquity of Ephraim is exposed and the wickedness of Samaria revealed; for they practice deceit, and a thief enters in [houses], bandits raid outside.**

Attaching the final part of 6:11 to 7:1, Hosea hears God express despair. Though God wants to "heal" all of Israel's problems (repeating the metaphor "heal," which is also used in 5:13, 6:1, and 14:5), God finds that Israel is still committing civil crimes, including thieves entering houses and robbers threatening people on the highway – both capital offenses. Rashi observes that at first, the evil people act in secret, but after becoming accustomed to criminality, they pursue their goals openly with a brazen disregard of consequences. Maimonides, who insisted that God has no human emotions, would remind readers to view the statement as a hyperbolic figure of speech.

2. **And let them not say to their heart. … I remember all their wickedness; now their own doings have beset them about, they are before my face.**

Hosea does not reveal what the people say, or more precisely, imagine, perhaps intentionally to emphasize that their views are so egregious that they, like other foul language, should not be spoken aloud. We are reminded of Genesis 4:8, where the Bible states "And Cain said to Abel his brother" – and then does not report Cain's angry words. Verse 2 emphasizes the callous fearlessness of the citizens, performing their deeds openly before man and God.

By "I remember," Hosea begins to enumerate ancient misdeeds as well as present ones (Olam Hatanakh).

3. **They delight the king with their wickedness and the commanders with their lies.**

Even the rulers of Israel are involved in the evil behaviors, perhaps gaining some monetary profits from it. Rather than attempting to control the ravaging masses, they delight in it. Rashi adds: the king wanted to see the evils in the land. Similarly, the Revised Standard Version translation of the Bible translates this verse as "By their wickedness they make the king glad, and the princes by their treachery." Some scholars suggest that *yesamchu*, "delight," should be read as *yimshechu*: "In their wickedness they anoint kings" (Interpreter's Bible).

4. **They are all adulterers, like an oven heated by a baker, who ceases to stir from the kneading of the dough until it is leavened.**

The Targum understands "adulterers" literally: "They all desire to commit adultery with the wives of their companions." However, adultery may be used here, as in past chapters, as a metaphor for the disregard of God. They abandoned God like adulterers, overheated in their shameless emotions, which burn within them like a roaring flame (also in Jeremiah 9:1, Proverbs 6:26–29, Job 31:12, and elsewhere). The term could also refer to the conspirators who plan to assassinate the king. They rest briefly from their audacities while waiting for the culmination of their plots (Kil). Ehrlich takes a similar approach to Kil, believing that adultery does not fit the context. He suggests that there is a scribal error and the text should have two words that were mistakenly combined: *min ophim*, "They were overheated."

5. **On the day of [the festival of] our king, the commanders made him sick with the heat of wine, [and] he joins hands with mockers.**

Kil notes that the king's inebriated state is an embarrassment, as indicated in Proverbs 31:4. He also understands "he joins hands with mockers" to mean that the king did not need the mockers' encouragement – he joined them, he pampered himself with wine. This is how the word *mashakh*, "join," is used in Ecclesiastes 2:3. The phrase may also imply that he joined hands in drunken revelry to dance. Olam Hatanakh notes that the Hebrew *lotzetzim* not only means "mockers" but also "evildoers."

Hosea seems to be alluding to a specific event which he does not identify. It may have been the coronation day of King Zechariah son of Jeroboam II after the latter's death (Targum, Rashi, ibn Ezra, Radak, Kara, and many others) or it may have been the king's birthday (Altschuler and Olam Hatanakh, which states that this is the view of most modern commentators). Not only did Israel's rulers and military commanders observe the event happily, they turned it into a drunken orgy, reflecting the shameless behavior of the citizenry. The nation's leaders were chosen by the king because they were scorners of morality; rather than protecting him, they enticed the king to overindulge until he became sick. He was so far removed from reality that even in his sickness he joined hands with the scorners.

Ehrlich rejects the notion that Hosea is speaking about the king's birthday, his installation, or the anniversary of his crowning because such days are celebrated not only in the palace, but by the entire nation. Also, Hosea would have seen nothing wrong in people celebrating these events. Ehrlich understands that the "day" was the day the plotters began to intoxicate the king, possibly over a period of several days, until they assassinated him.

6. **For they prepare their hearts like an oven, [while they approach him] with intrigue. Their baker sleeps all night; in the morning he blazes like a flaming fire.**

These same sycophants were burning with desire for a *coup d'état* against Zechariah. Their leader Shallum, a captain in Zechariah's army (the baker), assassinated him in front of the people after the king had ruled for only a month.[1] Shallum sleeps calmly on the night before the assassination, assured of success, but awakes in the morning ablaze with his vicious plot. The Hebrew word *opheihem*, translated here as "their baker," is understood as "anger" by the Targum; the word contains the same root as "oven."

The civil unrest and anarchy among the people was paralleled in the palace. Four of the six kings who followed Jeroboam II died as a result of assassinations. The six were Zechariah (assassinated), Shallum (assassinated), Menahem, Pekahiah (assassinated), Pekah (assassinated), and Hoshea, the last king of Israel.

7. **All of them are hot as an oven; they devour their judges. All their kings are fallen, and none of them calls to me.**

Shallum's assassination is not unique. Besides being followed by three others, only eight of Israel's seventeen kings, called here "judges," died a natural death. The remaining nine were either dethroned or murdered by their successors. "All their kings are fallen" is customary biblical hyperbole. Ehrlich connects the two final phrases: they are fallen because they did not call on me, meaning that they did not rule with civility, in accordance with the divine code.

It is characteristic of all the Targums to add the word "pray" to the text, so as to emphasize the importance of prayer, even though Scripture may only mention such acts as "calling," as it does here. Prayer is added here and in verses 10 and 14, as well as in 8:2.

The text uses the word "judges," here and in 13:10, probably signifying "leaders" of the army or of the people, as the word is used in the biblical book Judges. Rashi, however, takes the word literally: the people killed their Sanhedrin[2] because the judges criticized their behavior.

8. **Ephraim, he mixes with nations; Ephraim is a loaf not turned over.**

Hosea's "mixes" is unclear. It could denote marriages with non-Israelites, join-

---

1. See II Kings 15:10–16.

2. The word Sanhedrin is Greek and did not enter the Hebrew language until Judah came in contact with the Greeks in around 320 BCE. The rabbis considered it to be a supreme court of seventy-one members. See Sidney B. Hoenig, *The Great Sanhedrin* (Philadelphia: Dropsie College, 1953). See my review of this, my uncle's book, on Amazon.

ing in alliances with foreign nations, or incorporating alien culture. Ibn Ezra comments: since Hosea used the metaphor "oven" to depict the conspirators' plan, he continues its use here to portray its implementation. "A loaf not turned over" is a half-baked condition; another way of describing the aforementioned situation is that Shallum was assassinated after he assassinated Zechariah. The "loaf not turned over" could also denote that Israel is ruined, just as a loaf left on the fire burns and is not eatable.

9. **Foreigners sap his strength, but he does not realize it. His hair is sprinkled with gray, but he does not notice.**

Besides being half-baked, meaning that it lacks direction, the nation was sapped of its power and made into a vassal. Although time has passed ("hair sprinkled with gray"), neither the nation's leaders nor its people recognize how Israel has been diminished by foreign countries, like a weakened, senile old man (Radak).

10. **Israel's pride testifies against him, but despite all this they do not return to the Lord their God or search for him.**

Hosea repeats his depiction from 5:5. The "pride of Israel," meaning either its rulers or the people's arrogance, has led Israel astray. They do not realize that they must return to God. The term for "return" is *shavu*, the opposite of abandonment and adultery. This theme is repeated in many chapters and is dramatically developed in chapter 14. The rabbis see chapter 14 as describing the elaborate system of prayers involved in halakhic repentance. This is doubtful, however, for the concept did not exist at that time. See the commentary to 3:5 and the essay on repentance later in this book.

11. **Ephraim is like a silly dove, senseless. They call to Egypt; [then] they go to Assyria.**

Hosea gives examples of Israel mixing with nations, mentioned as a generality in verse 8. Israel flutters like a brainless dove, here and there, seeking help and security through alliances with Egypt and then with Assyria. Israel fails to realize that such alliances come with the allying nation assuming some control over Israel. When the Hasmonean brothers fought to rule Judea many centuries later, one brother sought aid from Pompey of Rome, which led to

Rome taking control of Judea and the destruction of the second temple. The mention of both Egypt and Assyria could be seen as evidence of pro-Egypt and pro-Assyria parties in Israel.

12. **When they go, I will throw my net over them; I will pull them down like the birds in the sky. I will chastise them as their community will hear.**

The metaphor of catching Israel in a net is an apt description of what follows alliances, as mentioned in the prior commentary. The resulting degradation of Israel will not only affect the nation's rulers, but even the people will bear it ("they will hear").

13. **Woe to them because they have strayed from me! Destruction to them, because they have rebelled against me! Should I redeem them even though they speak falsely about me?**

Hosea hears or imagines God lamenting the situation. God considers saving Israel, but is restrained because the people continue their incivility even as they perform what they think are pious works. See the essay "The Origin of Sin" later in this book for a definition of *pasha*, "rebelled."

14. **They have not cried out to me with their hearts but wail on their beds. They bestir themselves [to pray to me] for grain and new wine; they turn away from me.**

Their piety consists of self-seeking prayers for sustenance, and God disapproves of their deeds.

15. **I trained them and strengthened their arms, but they plot evil against me.**

The nation has forgotten its era of prosperity, which was brought about by God.

16. **They return, but not upwards; they are like a faulty bow. Their commanders will fall by the sword because of the rage of their tongues. This will be their ridicule in the land of Egypt."**

"Return," as noted previously, is a frequent refrain in Hosea, as is its opposite, the abandonment of God. See commentary to 3:5. Here, Hosea seems to be saying that the Israelites are reacting to their distress, but not by returning to God. Their misguided political maneuvers are like a faulty bow that is unable to reach its true target. As a result of their improper diplomacy ("the rage of their tongues"), the commanders will find themselves involved in war and will die. Egypt, from whom they sought support, will mock them for their foolish diplomacy (Olam Hatanakh).

Chapter 8

This chapter emphasizes that God desires to save Israel from the impending Assyrian attack, but is constrained because the nation continues its immorality. The chapter contains many repetitions and includes the ubiquitous obscurities. It has passages (such as verses 5–6) that can be interpreted to state that Israel offered sacrifices to idols, and others (especially verses 1 and 13) that indicate that the nation is offering sacrifices to God.

1.   **"Put the horn to your lips! As an eagle is over the house of the Lord, because they [the people] have broken my covenant and rebelled against my teaching.**

Hosea hears God instructing him to sound the alarm to warn Israel that the Assyrians, who are fierce like an eagle, are about to swoop down upon the nation because Israel has transgressed against the divine teachings. The Hebrew has *torah*, which even in the Five Books of Moses is used repeatedly to mean a "teaching," not a description of the five books. William Rainey Harper states: "Among the prophets *torah* = instruction, and refers to the admonition of the prophets.… In Deuteronomy *statutes and judgments* is the phrase which expresses the idea of law; while *torah* is still used of oral instruction."[1]

Rashi reads the verse as a call to Israel to "blow the shofar and repent."

---

1. In *A Critical and Exegetical Commentary on Amos and Hosea,* International Critical Commentary (Charles Scribner's Sons, 1905). Harper refers us to Isaiah 1:10, 2:3, 8:16, 42:4; Jeremiah 18:18, 26:4, 5; Ezekiel 7:26; Haggai 2:11; and Zechariah 7:12.

Some scholars translate *nesher* as vulture, a carrion bird that will be figuratively present at Israel's death (Interpreter's Bible).

If "house of the Lord" is taken literally, it would imply that Hosea felt that the temples in the northern kingdom were places where proper sacrifices were brought. Therefore, some commentators understand it to mean "land of Israel" (Olam Hatanakh).

See 7:13 where "rebelling" is mentioned, and the essay "The Origin of Sin" later in this book, for a definition of *pasha*, "rebelled."

2. **Will they cry out to me, 'Our God! We, Israel, know you'?**

Rashi explains that the word "Israel" is misplaced. The verse should read: "Will Israel cry out to me, 'Our God, we know you'?" The prophet's constant complaint is that Israel does not "know God," as in 2:10. He hears God wonder whether now that the people are facing disaster they will finally know God.

3. **[But] Israel has rejected what is good; [therefore] an enemy will pursue him.**

Israel will not change. *Zanach*, "reject" or "cast off," is ironically repeated in verse 7, where the prophet states that the calf that they hold has cast them off, just as they have cast off the good. The word "good" is a moral term and indicates that Israel is continuing to act immorally.

Some scholars read verse 2 as "Israel will cry to me: 'My God, we know you!'" Yet despite this cry, they continue their immoral conduct in verse 3.

4. **They set up kings without my consent; they choose commanders that I knew not [without my approval]. With their silver and their gold, they make images for themselves that they may be cut off [resulting in their own destruction].**

As indicated in chapter 7, Israel enthroned six kings within a short span of time. Virtually all seized the throne through assassinations and intrigue, which is contrary to the divine will. The Hebrew *atzabim* means "idols," as translated by the Jewish Publication Society, the Interpreter's Bible, and others. But *atzabim* also means "images," as I discuss in the commentary to 4:17. It is therefore unclear whether Hosea considers the images and calves to be idols, and scholars differ whether they were merely fetishes or idols. The Targum, for example, sees them as idols and, characteristically for the Targums, calls them *ta'avan*, "mistakes." It inserts the term in its translation four times in this chapter – in verses 4, 6, 11, and 14.

In contrast, Harper sees the images and calf in verse 5 as images of God and states that Hosea is the first prophet who "spoke against making images of Yahweh"; in doing so he would be reiterating the biblical prohibition again making and using images, as expressed in the Decalogue in Exodus 20:4 and Deuteronomy 5:8.[2] The *Encyclopaedia Judaica* also posits that Hosea does not speak against idol worship. It states that 9:10 and 13:1 refer to past misdeeds (Baal-peor or Ahab's Baal) and not the worship in Israel during the lifetime of Hosea, and that 4:17 is corrupt and should read "a band of lechers." Kil similarly understands that Hosea is not speaking of his generation here, but of Jeroboam I's reign. Jeroboam separated the ten tribes from the Judean kingdom and built temples in Beth-el and Dan, where he placed calves – which may not have been idols even though the biblical book Kings calls them so.[3] Hosea's failure to speak about idol worship in Israel is consistent with Amos's reticence on the topic.[4] See the essay on the golden calf later in this book.

The rulers' zeal was misplaced. While directed toward the fashioning of images or idols out of the gold and silver they could amass, it is unclear what they do with their wealth, and Hosea warns that what they are doing will result in the destruction of the nation and the exile of its people.

Jewish tradition has two views regarding kings.[5] I Samuel 8 and 12 expresses the view that from a theological perspective, the Israelites need no king

---

2. This command is generally ignored today. Although people arguably don't worship the images, Christians wear and kiss the cross and Jews do the same with a mezuzah or Star of David around their necks.

3. I Kings 12.

4. See my book *Jonah and Amos*, Unusual Bible Interpretations (Jerusalem: Gefen Publishing House, 2016).

5. Deuteronomy 17:14–20 speaks about what should occur when the people desire to have a king. Commentators disagree on how to interpret the section. Some, such as Maimonides, feel that it commands the people to have a king; Maimonides states that it was the 173rd biblical command. Others, such as Nachmanides, contend the section only allows a king, but the better behavior is not to have one. The prophet Samuel was opposed to the institution of a king, but he may have been driven by his feeling that the people were rejecting the leadership of his sons. See my *Who Was the Biblical Prophet Samuel?* (forthcoming) on I Samuel 8 for other citations.

because God is their king and their protector. The issue here is whether Hosea is agreeing with this opinion here and in 13:9–11, and is against any king. Olam Hatanakh states that many modern commentators hold this view. See also 10:9.

5. **Samaria, your calf is cast off! My anger burns against them. How long will they be incapable of purity?**

See verse 3 regarding the ironic use of "cast off." Rashi and others translate the final phrase: "How long will they be defiled; when will they be clean?" Kil suggests that "clean" here may also denote "innocent" of wrong, as in a court case.

Jeroboam I broke off from the kingdom of King Rehoboam, grandson of King David, and established a new nation in the north called Israel for the rebelling ten tribes. He built two temples in the north, in Beth-el and Dan, and decorated them with calves, perhaps at the temples' entrance.[6] While the books of Kings and Chronicles, written by Judean enemies of Israel, called the calves idols, scholars are unsure whether this is true. They could have been used as pedestals, as other nations used such figures (McKeating). There is no indication that the prophets who berated the people for their misconduct in the north considered them to be idols.

Hosea mentions Samaria, which was the capital of Israel. He states that God is angry with the calf. This verse may be using a different metaphor to return to the oft-discussed theme of the people's inappropriate worship. The people act in a manner that they think is pious. They bring sacrifices to God, as indicated in verse 13. But, as stated in 6:6, God wants Israel to be civil. Thus the calves, symbols of their misplaced piety, will be destroyed with the kingdom. The word translated as "purity" (*nikayon*) also means "clean"; the calves will be bereft of fetishistic notions. However, see the next passage.

6. **It is from Israel! A craftsman made it. It is not God. The calf of Samaria will be broken in pieces.**

There is a problem with verses 5 and 6, which speak of the calf of Samaria. We have no idea what the calf of Samaria is. The verses speak of a calf in the singular and seem to state that it is in the capital Samaria. Yet we know that Jeroboam

---

6. I Kings 12.

I set calves, plural, in Beth-el and Dan. Samaria was not even built when he did so. It is possible that Hosea is using the calf as a description of Samaria. Additionally, verses 5 and 6 do not follow verse 4, which speaks of the kings and commanders, an idea resumed in verse 7. Furthermore, it seems that Hosea believes that the Israelites are offering sacrifices to God, as stated explicitly in verse 13. Thus, 5 and 6 do not seem to belong in the chapter. Scholars maintain that parts of Hosea were added to the author's book after his death and after the destruction of Israel, and the editors inserted these verses to belittle Israel.[7] It may therefore be that Hosea was either speaking of the calf as a symbol, not as an idol, or that the two passages are Judean adulterations of the book.

The phrase "it is not God" could be understood as "it is an idol," even though the book does not state this explicitly. McKeating believes the calves were not seen as idols. "The idolater was no more likely to equate his image with his god than the Christian to equate his crucifix with Christ." See 13:2 which is similar. It may be that the prophet is saying "the calf, which can be seen as a symbol of the nation, is not holy. It represents what God abhors."[8]

Radak understands that "It is from Israel" is stating that Israel did not copy the calves of other nations, but copied the golden calf that the Israelites had Aaron, Moses's brother, make after they left Egyptian bondage. Although not discussed here by Radak, many scholars and rabbis felt that the golden calf was not an idol, but a misguided representation of God. It was a fetish or image, and all images are prohibited in the Decalogue.

7. **For they sow the wind and reap the whirlwind. It has no stalk. The bud will yield no flour. Were it to yield [grain], foreigners would swallow it up.**

Hosea, like many prophets, likes figurative language and metaphors. Here he uses four different ones to describe how the attacked people will be destroyed.

---

7. See the introduction, which discusses why numerous kings of Judah are mentioned in verse 1 even though Hosea's mission was in the north. Some scholars insist that the parts throughout this book that mention Judah were added by Judeans.

8. Exodus 20:21 prohibits Israelites from using instruments to chisel the rocks that would be used for the altar. Rashbam explains that the Israelite temptation to copy the religious pagan practices necessitated the command that the stone altar be crafted without iron instruments, lest the craftsman be tempted to chisel artistic – and unacceptable – images into the stones.

More will follow in the next verses. The similar phrase "They that sow in tears shall reap in joy" is in Psalms 126:5.

8. **Israel is swallowed up; now she is among the nations like a vessel no one wants.**

This is most likely a prediction rather than a report of Israel's destruction, with the ten tribes disappearing to become known as "the ten lost tribes." McKeating sees the description of the conquered nation as proof that this passage must have been composed in Judah after 722 BCE.

9. **For they have gone up to Assyria like a wild donkey wandering alone. Ephraim has sold herself to lovers.**

Although Israel bribed Assyria to come and help the nation, Assyria will come and destroy it, and Israel will wander outside its demolished land like a wild, lost donkey. King Menahem[9] and later King Hoshea, Israel's last king, tried to buy Assyrian support.

Ehrlich proposes that it is Assyria that is described as a "wild donkey" – a nation that is unreliable and interested only in itself, and despite any treaty is untrustworthy and will wander off alone.

10. **Although they have sold themselves among the nations, I will now gather them together. They will begin to waste away under the burden [oppression] of king [and] commanders.**

This is another way of saying what has already been said. Israel thought it could gain peace and security by buying help from Assyria, but instead of lightening the load of fear and disquiet, Assyria will become a burden to it, causing many citizens to die and the nation to diminish.

11. **For Ephraim built many altars for sin [offerings], these have become altars for sinning.**

The first part of this passage could be translated negatively, as done by Lehrman and the Jewish Publication Society (JPS): "For Ephraim hath multiplied altars to sin." This implies that the altars are for idols, although this contradicts verse 13. In contrast, the verse can be seen to imply "offerings" and express the same

9. See commentary to 5:13.

irony found in prior verses: Israel thought it was acting properly by offering sacrifices to God, but, as stated in the next passage, they did not do what God required. This is similar to how Nyberg translates it: "Though Ephraim has made many altars to take away sin, yet they have become for them altars for sinning."[10]

12. I wrote for them many of my teachings, but they regarded them as something foreign.

The prophet repeats his message of verse 1 and emphasizes that Israel has no excuse; God taught them ethical teachings. As mentioned previously, the word *torah* is used in the Five Books of Moses and elsewhere in the Bible to mean a particular "teaching," not the Five Books of Moses.

The word translated "I wrote" actually appears in the future tense in the Hebrew: *ekhtov*. The Bible very frequently uses the future when it means the past, and the singular when it means the plural, and vice versa.

When and how did God teach ethical lessons? Hosea does not say. It is possible that he is referring to himself or the several prophets who spoke the divine message at the time – Amos, Micah, Isaiah, and Jonah (Rashi, Altschuler, and others). Radak states that the text uses the future tense "I will write" to indicate a continuous process in which the prophets frequently warn the people. It may be, as Maimonides teaches, that nature teaches these lessons. McKeating writes: "The text is an interesting witness to the existence of written codes of law." It is also possible that the phrase "they regarded them as something foreign" is ironic: even foreign nations know the ethical lessons, although they do not practice all of them all the time, but Israel ignores them and devoutly states, as many self-righteous religious Jews argue today, that they will not copy the ideas of foreigners.

13. They offer sacrifices of fire to me, they sacrifice and eat the meat, the Lord is not pleased with them. Now he will remember their wickedness and punish their iniquity. They will return to Egypt.

Lehrman and JPS translate: "As for the sacrifices that are made by fire to me,

---

10. H. S. Nyberg, *Studien zum Hosea Buch* (Uppsala: Lundequistaka, 1935). Nyberg is quoted in the Interpreter's Bible.

let them sacrifice flesh and eat it." Since Lehrman and JPS contend that Israel worshipped idols, this translation implies that despite the overwhelming number of sacrifices being made as pagan worship, a few may have been directed to God. However, the text does not say "as for" and "let them." Hosea is saying: "I recognize that the sacrifices are dedicated to God, but proper sacrifices are not enough to please God because, as stated frequently in this chapter and in 6:6, it is proper interpersonal relations that God desires." As Ehrlich writes, God is saying: "Stop preparing meat for me. I do not want it. Eat it yourselves."

Hosea makes ironic use of the oft-repeated refrain "return" in the phrase "they will return to Egypt": God wants the people to cease their adulterous-type activities and return to God, but since they do not want to return to God, they will return to Egypt. Like many other statements in the chapter, this phrase should be understood as a figure of speech, here meaning exile and enslavement. The Septuagint adds "and among the Assyrians they will eat unclean food," which is in our text in 9:3, and which parallels the opening of the verse, "they sacrifice and eat the meat."

The practice of Israelites eating the bulk of the sacrifice and giving the priests only parts of it is dramatized in I Samuel 1:4–5, where Elkanah, who later becomes the father of the prophet Samuel, shares a sacrifice with his family.

14. Israel has forgotten their maker and built palaces. Judah has fortified many towns. But I will send fire on their cities that will consume their castles."

The prophet repeats his messages of 2:15 that Israel has forgotten God. God gave the nation prosperity (as in 2:10), and – as a result of the people's abandonment – Israel and Judah will be destroyed (as in 5:12, 8:4, and 8:8). Knowledge of God is a constant theme in Hosea, as in 2:22, 4:1, 4:6, 4:22, 6:3, 6:6, 7:9, and 8:3. It also appears as God making known, as in 5:9; God remembering, as in 5:3 and 7:2; being "revealed" to God in 7:1, and Israel "forgetting" God, as in 2:15 and this passage; and as lack of understanding, as in 4:14.

As mentioned in the book's introduction, many commentators feel certain that the book of Hosea was edited in Judah after the fall of Israel in 722 BCE, and the editors introduced statements about Judah into the book. Some of them think that "Judah has fortified many towns" here is such an insertion, since Judah is not mentioned elsewhere in the chapter. Others who support this view say that the Judeans changed "Ephraim has fortified many towns," which fits the context, to "Judah," which does not.[11]

---

11. Ironically, according to these scholars this book which speaks about adultery has itself been adulterated.

Chapter 9

In chapter 9, the prophet foretells what will occur during the Israelites' exile from their land. The abundance they experienced during the era of Jeroboam II will end. But as usual, Hosea gives little details and speaks in generalities. An exception and of special interest is verse 4, which has an unexpected detail – one that the rabbis would reject when the second temple was destroyed in 70 CE. Hosea speaks about the people sacrificing to God while in foreign lands, offerings that the deity rejects. Also worthy of attention is verse 10, which raises the question again whether the prophet knew about the existence of the Five Books of Moses.

1. **"Do not rejoice Israel unto exaltation, as other people: for you have gone a whoring from your God, you loved a harlot's hire upon every corn floor.**

Israel should not be optimistic or see their period of prosperity as a time of rejoicing. Other nations may rejoice in their bounty, but Israel has no cause for joy. It will soon see punishment, for the nation deserted God; they were like prostitutes who shamelessly engage in sex whenever possible, even on the corn floor. The Targum, as usual, uses this verse, 8, and 13 to state again that Israel is worshipping idols. Kara, Altschuler, Radak, and ibn Ezra mention the worship of idols in verse 1.

Without any textual support, Julius Wellhausen suggested that the oracle in this chapter was spoken by Hosea on the occasion of a great festival which was bacchanalian, enjoyed with overindulgence in wine and much sex. The Interpreter's Bible quotes him and adds that the festivity was dedicated to Baal, was made merry with sex on the threshing floor, and was performed "in the hope that by this service they would ensure for themselves the fruits of the field." Hosea tells his countrymen that "it is these fruits which will fail them, so that the worthlessness of Baal service will be made manifest."

In contrast, Jewish commentators say Hosea spoke these words during the holiday of Succoth, the holiday celebrating the conclusion of the harvest. They base this view on verse 5's use of the word *chag*, meaning "holiday" and "celebration." *Chag* is the noun used in the Bible for Succoth since this holiday was the most festive, because after the harvest ended many people were able to leave their fields and attend the temple, thank God for the harvest, and celebrate their bounty.

Ehrlich explains the opening words as "you will be unable to celebrate" because you will be defeated in war and exiled from Israel. He also contends that the verse is not speaking about idol worship, but Hosea is reflecting the idea that joining other nations or copying their practices is like idol worship.

2. **The threshing floor and the winepress will not feed them, and the new wine will fail her.**

While the land is currently yielding abundant crops, the time is coming when this yield will cease.

3. **They will not dwell in the land of the Lord; but Ephraim will return to Egypt, and they will eat unclean things in Assyria.**

Israel will be unable to live off its land because the people will be driven into exile, which is the meaning of the metaphor "return to Egypt," as in 8:13. Since the Israelites polluted their sacrifices to God by following the sacrifices with immoral acts against fellow citizens, once in exile they will eat "unclean things" – the opposite of sacrificial meat. Hosea is the first prophet to use the term "the land of the Lord" (Kil).

4. **They will not pour wine offerings to the Lord, neither will they be pleasing to him: their sacrifices will be to them as the bread of mourners; all that eat it will be polluted, for their bread will be for themselves. It will not come into the house of the Lord.**

This is a difficult passage. Read together with verse 3, it is obvious that the prophet is speaking about the nation of Israel in exile. Hosea seems to believe that even in exile the people will be permitted to offer sacrifices to God. The Targum, Rashi, and Kara accept that the verse is speaking of sacrifices to God.

This bothered some commentators because when the Jerusalem temple was destroyed in 70 CE, the rabbis ruled that sacrifices must be discontinued; they felt that the sacrifices may only be brought in the temple in Jerusalem.[1] Hosea, some eight hundred years earlier, seems to disagree. He appears to be saying that although the exiles will make sacrifices to God while they are in Assyria, God will not delight in the sacrifices. God will consider the offerings polluted because of their misdeeds, like the meager foods eaten by mourners – not food for God, but food for the one who offers it.

Many solutions to this problem were offered, such as the following: (1) Altschuler supposes that this verse refers to Judea. (2) Ibn Ezra presumes the verse speaks about Israelites who were not exiled, who offered sacrifices in Israel. (3) Radak asserts that the prophet is talking of offerings made by Israelites before the destruction and exile. (4) Kil speculates that the passage is saying, "If you wanted to sacrifice outside of Israel, God would not accept the offering." (5) Ehrlich, Olam Hatanakh, the Interpreter's Bible and others contend that there is a scribal error and that the prophet is not saying that sacrifices will be brought to God in Assyria or Egypt. Based on G. R. Driver,[2] they suggest that we should read *yei'arkhu* instead of *ye'ervu*, substituting a *khaf* for the biblical *vet*, and translate "they will not offer their sacrifices to him." (6) McKeating is similar and translates: "They shall pour out no wine to the Lord, they shall not bring their sacrifices to him."

Actually, the basic premise to this discussion is faulty. While it is true that sacrifices ceased after the destruction of the second temple in 70 CE – not because of being outside of Israel, but because the temple in which they were brought was destroyed – we know that sacrifices were offered outside of Israel even much later than the time of Hosea. The Aramean captain Naaman offered sacrifices to God in Aram, although he placed earth from Israel under

---

1. It is also possible that the rabbis realized, as Maimonides would write in his *Guide of the Perplexed* 3:32 much later, that God did not need or even want sacrifices and only "allowed" them. It may be that the rabbis saw the destruction of the temple as a good opportunity to put an end to sacrifices, as it provided a rationale that people could accept.
2. Quoted in the Interpreter's Bible.

his altar, and the Israelite prophet did not tell him this was prohibited.[3] Also, Jews established two temples in Egypt during the second temple period, in Leontopolis and Honio.[4]

The difficulty aside, it should be noted that it is clear that the offering, wherever made, is directed to God, and not an idol. The reason for this could be that the Israelites had always made sacrifices to God, or that while they had sacrificed to idols in the past, they now faced their problems and turned to God.

It should also be noted that the phrase "not come into the house of the Lord" should not be understood literally for, as indicated in verse 3, the prophet is describing the offerings of the exiles; it means "although the offerings are directed toward God, God will not accept them."

The term *l'naphsham* has at its root the word *nefesh*, which means "soul" in modern Hebrew. It did not have this meaning in the Bible, but meant "a person," as in Leviticus 2:1 which speaks of a *nefesh* bringing a sacrifice.

5. **What will you do in the appointed season, and in the day of the feast of the Lord?**

The people will no longer be able to enjoy the festive days as they did in their own land. Radak and Rashi construe the appointed season and day of the feast of the Lord as the day that the nations will destroy Israel, while Olam Hatanakh supposes it is Succoth.

6. **For, lo, they are gone because of destruction. Egypt will gather them up. Memphis will bury them. Their precious treasures of silver – nettles will possess them; thorns will be in their tents.**

Hosea builds on his metaphor for exile which he began in 8:3–4 and verse 3

---

3. II Kings 5:17.

4. Babylonian Talmud, *Megillah* 10a, and Tosaphot there (s.v. *shamati*); Josephus, *Antiquities* 13:13 and *Wars of the Jews* 7:2–4; Kil; and Olam Hatanakh. The cited Talmudic section speaks of the allowance of sacrifices during the period of *heteir habamot*, "the time when altars were allowed," which may be an anachronism. It assumes that Jewish law, or more specifically the rabbis, allowed altars outside of the central temple before the temple was built. The problem with this view is that rabbis did not exist during this period and there was no legal system about restricting temples during this time mentioned in any ancient source. It seems that *heteir habamot* was a later invention to justify the behavior of the Israelite ancestors.

of this chapter. He states that though some Israelite survivors will make their way to Egypt, the land in which Israel placed their trust for aid and safety, it will become the site of their burial. Memphis was a city just south of Cairo and used as a place of burial (Lehrman). The survivors rushed in such haste from Israel that they left their wealth behind. The rush to Egypt happened after the second temple was destroyed in 70 CE and Gedaliah, the governor of Judea appointed by Rome, was assassinated, as related in II Kings 25:26.

The Israelites will leave behind their many possessions during their escape to Egypt – so much, that the enemy will ignore much of it.

7. **The days of visitation are come, the days of recompense are come; Israel will know it. The prophet is a fool, the man of spirit is mad, because of the multitude of your iniquity, the hatred is great.**

Hosea foresees that the prophesied destruction will occur, clearly visible to all. It is only then that the people will realize that the false prophets who predicted a continuance of prosperity were fools, or it may be that Hosea is quoting what people said about him when they rejected his warnings. When the enemy attacks, their hatred of Israel will express itself in brutality.

It is possible, but by no means certain, that when he speaks of a prophet being a fool, Hosea is referring to Jonah of II Kings 14 who advised Jeroboam II to expand his territory.

8. **The watchman of Ephraim is with my God: but a snare of a fowler is in all his ways, and hatred in the house of his God.**

This verse is impossible to decipher with any degree of certainty. It is possible that Hosea is drawing a contrast between himself, a true prophet, and the false prophets mentioned in the prior passage. Although he sees himself as a watchman over Ephraim, appointed to this mission by God, the people – not least the priests in the house of God – have set a snare in his path. In a similar vein, Amos has a confrontation with Amaziah the priest of Beth-el, who hated him (Amos 7).

It should be noted that Hosea is calling the temples of Israel "house[s] of God," which is another indication that he thought that worship there was directed to God.

9. **They have deeply corrupted themselves, as in the days of Gibeah. He will remember their iniquity. He will punish their misdeeds.**

The prophet mentions Gibeah here and in 10:9, but neither this book nor the Targum explains the critique. Rashi clarifies that it either refers to the crowning of Saul described in I Samuel 10–12, with the verse expressing God's displeasure that the people insisted on having a king instead of relying on God, or to Judges 19–21 where the Bible tells the terrible, unforgivable tale that began in Gibeah with rape. The rape was followed by a civil war between Israelite tribes, in which virtually the entire tribe of Benjamin was wiped out; they were saved when other tribes allowed the Benjamite survivors to kidnap and rape hundreds of defenseless women.[5] Ibn Ezra, Radak, Kara, Kil, and Altschuler presume the verse refers to the latter option. See also verse 15 and 10:9.

Is Hosea saying that descendants will be punished for their ancestors' deeds? If so, modern readers would argue that this is unethical.[6] However, he may be saying that the current behavior in Israel is as shocking as what occurred in Gibeah. If so, and it appears that this is the true interpretation, this is a huge overstatement.

10. **I found Israel like grapes in the wilderness. I saw your fathers as the first ripe in the fig tree at her first season. But they came to Baal-peor, and separated themselves unto that shame, and became detestable like that which they loved.**

Hosea continues to focus on past incidences, in this verse moving several hundred years before the Gibeah atrocity. He describes the divine love when the Israelites left Egypt and became a nation. He uses the metaphor of grapes, a tasty and refreshing fruit, as indicated in Micah 7:1. Grapes do not grow in the desert; one who sees such a thing would consider it miraculous, certainly a joyous occasion. The metaphor refers to the time when God demonstrated love for Israel by repeatedly saving them with miracles and by revealing the Decalogue. But Israel showed a lack of gratitude, rejected God, and worshipped the idol Baal-peor, as narrated in Numbers 23:28f, 25:18, and 31:16.

---

5. See the horrendous story in my book *Judges* in this series (Jerusalem: Gefen Publishing House, 2015).
6. See Exodus 20:5 and Deuteronomy 5:9.

Hosea mentions the Israelites' atrocious behavior at Baal-peor, at Gibeah where there was rape leading to civil war, and at Gilgal, where the nation ceased relying on God and insisted on crowning a king to save them. Yet it is significant that Hosea does not speak about the episode of the golden calf and the constant complaints by the Israelites to Moses demanding meat and water. Is this an indication that the prophet did not know about these events, because the Torah did not exist at that time? This question was also asked in the introduction to chapter 4, where we saw that Hosea did not include all of the commands of the Decalogue. The question is supported by Hosea's failure to critique his people for not observing the biblical commands, such as the Sabbath and holidays.

Rashi and Ehrlich postulate that the verse's final phrase reads: "they became detestable because of love" – meaning that the Israelites had sex with the female temple prostitutes of Baal-peor.

11. **Ephraim is like a bird whose glory will fly away; [there will be] no birth, no womb, and no conception.**

Once a glorious nation, Ephraim's grandeur will dissipate as a result of their corruption, speedily like a bird in flight. Along with other punishments, there will be a catastrophic decline in their birthrate, which may be a literal prediction or a metaphor emphasizing that their glory will be stripped from them. Alternatively, the prophet may be declaring that Ephraim will be dispersed and disappear like a frightened bird that flies away (Kil).

12. **Though they bring up their children, yet I will bereave them, so that no man will be left. Yea, woe also to them when I depart from them.**

If they do have children or, treating children metaphorically, have achievements, they will be short-lived. Rather than portraying God anthropomorphically moving, the Targum has the Shekhina do so.[7]

13. **Ephraim (as I saw Tyre) is planted in a pleasant place; but Ephraim will bring out his children to the murderer."**

The parenthetical phrase is Hosea's reflection on his personal observation, as

---

7. See commentary to 5:6 regarding the meaning of Shekhina.

the next verse is his own vexation. He recalls that Tyre was a beautiful city until it was destroyed, as Israel will be destroyed.[8] Israel will recruit its young to fight, but they will die in the war (Radak).

14. Give them, Lord, whatever you will give them. Give them a miscarrying womb and dry breasts.

Hosea seems to interrupt God's words here to express his exasperation. This is similar to Jacob's excited interruption during his deathbed description of his sons in Genesis 49:18, "I wait for your salvation, Lord." But while Jacob generally glanced forward to a favorable future, our prophet is seeking vengeance.

Some commentaries, such as the Interpreter's Bible, read this verse as a dialogue: "Give them, Lord...." "What will you give?" "Give them a miscarrying womb and dry breasts." The first statement is the beginning of an interrupted prayer; in the second God asks the prophet to suggest an appropriate punishment. The third is Hosea's answer. Rashi, ibn Ezra, and Radak view the entire verse as Hosea's prayer. Rashi speculates that Hosea is wishing that the children die while young, for mourning over a baby, he contends, is not as great as mourning over an adult.

Ephraim means "fruitful," but the frustrated prophets want the nation to experience the opposite.

15. "All their wickedness is in Gilgal, for there I hated them; because of the wickedness of their doings I will drive them from my house. I will love them no more; all their leaders are rebellious.

This is a repeat of oracles stating that Israel acted improperly and will be punished. Gilgal is mentioned in 4:15 and will reappear in 12:11. Gilgal was the place where (1) Saul, Israel's first king was proclaimed;[9] (2) Saul disobeyed God's command to destroy Amalek;[10] and (3) Baal worship was practiced, according to some commentators but without any biblical proof.[11] It was also (4) the first settlement of the Israelites after crossing into Canaan during

---

8. See Isaiah 23.
9. I Samuel 11:14.
10. I Samuel 13:5–14, 15:12–33.
11. The Interpreter's Bible, Radak, and Rashi.

the days of Joshua, and as such Israel should be thankful to God rather than abandoning the deity.[12]

"House" either refers to temples, which would confirm that there were temples dedicated to the true God, or is a synecdoche for the land of Israel, as in 8:1. Alternatively, as Ehrlich surmises, God declares: "I will no longer be your God and you will not be my people."

Ephraim is smitten, their root is dried up, they will bear no fruit. Even if they bring forth, yet will I slay even the beloved fruit of their womb.

This vision repeats from verses 2 and 14.

16. My God will cast them away because they did not listen to him: and they will be wanderers among the nations."

Hosea divines that the nation will have no settled homeland during the exile. The Hebrew word for "wanderers" (*nodedim*) is also used to describe Cain's punishment for killing his brother Abel in Genesis 1:12. The Targum replaces the anthropomorphism of Israel hearing God's voice with "they did not listen to his *memra*" – meaning God's "word," "command," or "wisdom."

---

12. Ibn Ezra.

Chapter 10

Chapter 10 continues the oft-stated prediction that Israel will be punished for its wrong behavior. It speaks about altars and pillars, but it is unclear whether the altars and pillars are devoted to God or idols.

---

1. **"Israel is a luxuriant vine; he brings forth fruit bountifully. As his fruit increased, he increased altars; the more goodly his land, the more goodly his pillars.**

   As usual, most of the images in the chapter are obscure. Hosea may be reflecting upon Israel's current bountiful situation or, on the contrary, rebuking his nation for wasting and misusing its prosperity. The patriarchs erected pillars, mentioned in 3:4 as instruments for worship of God, just as they used altars.[1] Pillars were later proscribed.[2] It is uncertain if pillars were forbidden during the time of Hosea. If they were allowed, this would be a positive description – the nation was worshipping God. If they were not allowed, the prophet would be saying that the nation lavished their prosperity upon forbidden objects. In any event, the text does not unambiguously say that the pillars were used for idol worship, although the Targum states "they worship at their *heathen* altars…they improved their *cult* pillars" and repeats these words in verse 2.

2. **Their heart is divided; now they will bear their guilt: he will break down their altars, he will spoil their pillars.**

---

1. Genesis 31:45, 35:20; II Samuel 18:18; Isaiah 19:19.
2. Exodus 34:13, 23:24; Leviticus 26:1; Deuteronomy 7:5, 12:3, 16:22.

By "divided," the prophet may be indicating that the people worship both God and idols. However, he is more likely recapping verse 6:6 – while the people sacrifice to God, they act uncivilly with one another.

3. **For now, they will say, 'We have no king, because we do not fear the Lord; what then will a king do for us?'**

Since Israel had kings, Hosea is most likely describing God as the king and imagining that the people are saying: "Since we do not fear God, and since help comes from God, it is as if we have no king, and no help."

4. **They speak words, they swear falsely, they make covenants; thus judgment springs up as hemlock in the furrows of the field.**

This verse may be describing the king and his ministers, who assure their subjects that they will give the nation security – but without God, these are idle words. Alternatively, the verse may be depicting people who speak about worshipping God but mistreat others, as in 6:6. Despite the abundance from their fields, these behaviors will lead to death.

Covenants may refer to political alliances or to the false assurances that the people give other citizens. The Targum clarifies: "They speak words of violence, they swear falsely, they make empty covenants."

5. **The inhabitants of Samaria will fear because of the calves of Beth-aven: for the people thereof will mourn over it, and the priests thereof who rejoiced over it, for its glory, because it is departed from it.**

Beth-aven, meaning "house of iniquity," is a disparaging epithet for Beth-el, as in 4:15. This passage may therefore be stating that Israel will be destroyed because they worshipped the calves in Beth-el, as the Targum maintains. It may also be recapping 6:6 – the worship in Beth-el, although directed toward God, is unacceptable because sacrifices should teach people how to behave with one another, but that did not occur in Beth-el. If the latter, the calves would be a symbol, a synecdoche, for the beautiful temple. When the people and priests see the calves and other temple objects being appropriated by the Assyrians they will mourn over the loss of what was precious to them. Radak clarifies that Hosea does not mention the second temple established by Jeroboam I in Dan, since Beth-el was the principle temple of Israel. See the essay on the golden calf later in this book.

The noun for priest, *komeir*, is usually reserved for pagan priests. This is its first appearance in Scripture. It is later found in II Kings 23:5 and Zephaniah 1:4. It is the second derogatory term in the passage, the first being when the prophet referred to Beth-el as Beth-aven. The prophet also employs the feminine form for calves, instead of the customary masculine, apparently a third disparagement.

6. **It will also be carried to Assyria as a present to King Contentious. Ephraim will receive shame, and Israel will be ashamed of his own counsel.**

The king of Assyria is referred to as King Contentious in 5:13 as well; see the commentary there. As they are thrust into exile, Israel will realize that they acted foolishly, relying on their own strategies and ignoring Hosea's warnings.

7. **As for Samaria, her king is cut off, as foam upon water.**

Israel's king and his kingdom will dissipate, like foam on water that rapidly evaporates.

8. **The high places also of Aven, the misdeed of Israel, will be destroyed; thorn and thistle will come up on their altars; and they will say to the mountains, 'Cover us'; and to the hills, 'Fall on us.'**

The Targum and Rashi identify Aven, "wickedness," as Beth-el. "Thorn and thistle" is mentioned in the punishment of Adam for eating the forbidden fruit in Genesis 3:18. "Cover us" and "fall on us" may be desperate suicidal wishes for death to avoid the pain and shame of exile. Ehrlich suggests that Israel may want the altars covered because they were the source of their disgrace. The Targum, as usual, labels the altars "heathen altars."

9. **Israel acted improperly from the days of Gibeah; there they stood; no battle in Gibeah occurred against the arrogant children.**

This verse could be construed in the following ways: (1) Just as the rapes and civil war began in Gibeah with the idol made by Micah (Judges 17), this same idol worship continues until today (Rashi). (2) The same immoral conduct shown by the rapes and war is continuing. They were not punished sufficiently for the rapes and civil war. They will be punished now. (3) Since the prophet speaks against the king in verses 3 and 7, and since he mentions that kings were set up without God's consent in 8:4, this verse may refer to Israel's first king, Saul, who came from Gibeah (Targum). When the people requested a king Samuel replied that the people should rely on God instead (I Samuel 10–12), and ultimately Saul was rejected by God and Samuel when he acted improperly during the war with Amalek (I Samuel 10–12, 15). (4) The prophet is saying that the people of his generation deserve a greater punishment than those who participated in the events at Gibeah because the latter had few prophets to warn them how to behave but his generation had many prophets to whom they should have listened (Ehrlich, who translates "Israel acted more improperly than [the people of] Gibeah").

10. **When I desire, I will chastise them, and nations will gather against them, when they bind themselves in their two furrows.**

No definite time is identified for when the future destruction will occur. It will happen when God wills it. The plural "nations" is used here despite the prediction of only Assyria attacking; perhaps because Assyria brought along mercenaries from allied nations. The "two furrows," also translated "two rings," is obscure and may designate (1) both Israel and Judah being destroyed (Ehrlich); (2) Israel's foolish attempt to secure an alliance with Assyria and Egypt; (3) the two calves in Beth-el and Dan; (4) plowing with two bulls, implying that despite attempting to strengthen their military (as farmers plow with two, not just a single bull), the country will be defeated and destroyed; or (5) the two misdeeds at Gibeah, one in Judges and one in Samuel.

11. **Ephraim is a heifer that is taught, and loves to thresh; but I passed over upon her fair neck. I will make Ephraim to ride; Judah will plow, and Jacob will break his clods.**

Ehrlich reasons that the Israelites' heifers enjoy plowing because their owners do not muzzle them but allow them to eat what they are threshing.[3] Understood negatively, Hosea is reiterating 8:12 – Israel was taught proper conduct, but rejected the teachings. God had not punished Israel in the past ("passed over her fair neck"), but will now cause the nation that preferred easy work to

---

3. As indicated in Deuteronomy 25:4.

suffer, to be symbolically like a heifer that must pull heavy equipment, plow hard ground, and crush clods of soil. However, Kara and others hear Hosea saying that God could give Ephraim and Judah power over the foreign nations (ride and plow them), while Altschuler sees the prophet speaking about the Lord giving Torah and *mitzvot*.

Since the plowing and crushing clods could be seen as the same activity, and since the prophet is usually addressing Israel and not Judah, the reference to Judah may be a scribal Judean insertion, as discussed in the next commentary and the book's introduction (Interpreter's Bible).

12. **Sow to yourselves in righteousness, reap in mercy; break up your fallow ground, for it is time to seek the Lord, until he comes and rains righteousness upon you.**

Continuing the agricultural metaphor of the previous two verses, Hosea cajoles his people to work the ground (their lives) properly and, as a result, God will respond with a good harvest, in contrast to what is predicted in verse 6 and in a multitude of other passages. The three items in verse 12 do not match precisely with the three in verse 11. "Sow" and "break the fallow ground" do parallel "ride" and "break the clods," but "reap" is not the same as "plow." This supports the view that "Judah will plow" is a Judean insertion, as indicated in the prior commentary and the introduction.

13. **You plowed wickedness, you reaped iniquity, you ate the fruit of lies; because you trusted in your way, in your many mighty men.**

The Israelites ignored Hosea's call in verse 12 and continued the practices of 11, relying on their own assessments and depending on human strength rather than God. The "mighty men" may be Assyria and Egypt, or the power of Israel's armed forces.

14. **Therefore, a tumult will arise among your people, and all your fortresses will be spoiled, as Shalman spoiled Beth-arbel in the day of battle; the mother was dashed in pieces with her children.**

It is uncertain who Shalman is. He may be Shalmaneser IV of Assyria, whose exploits are described in II Kings 17:3, or he may be another Assyrian king or military commander (Lehrman).[4] Beth-arbel is a town in the Galilee, but the battle there is not identified. The Targum treats Shalman as *shalom*, "peace," and as a general statement not referring to a specific event: "as the peaceful are plundered in an ambush on the day of battle [when] mothers and children are killed."

15. So has Beth-el done to you because of your great wickedness. In a morning the king of Israel will be utterly cut off."

Although the precise time of the Assyrian onslaught is not foretold, this passage says it will occur suddenly, after a night of improper behavior. Symbolically, the king will be killed at daybreak. The term "king of Israel" may be referring to the last king of Israel, Hoshea, or it may be a synecdoche for the oft-repeated prediction that the nation will be terminated.

The Septuagint substitutes "house of Israel" instead of Beth-el, and many scholars propose we should read "in the storm" in place of "in the morning." The change is an *ayin* instead of a *chet* (Interpreter's Bible). Ehrlich argues that both changes are correct.

---

4. The Interpreter's Bible contends that Shalman is not Shalmaneser III, IV, or V, but Salamanu of Moab who invaded Gilead during the eighth century.

Chapter 11

Hosea repeats his themes in this chapter using new and obscure metaphors. He expresses God's love of Israel in verses 1, 4, and 8–11, and Israel's rejection of this love in 2, 3, and 7. Hosea repeats some of the good things God did for Israel in the past despite Israel's rejection of God. And as in chapter 3, where God yearns for the return of adulterous Israel, these feelings are reiterated here where the prophet restates the oft-used word shuv, "return," four times in this chapter (5, 7, 9, and 11) and four times in the next (3, 7, 10, and 15).

Significantly, in verse 8 Admah and Zeboim are mentioned, but not Sodom and Gomorrah, the two cities mentioned as being destroyed in Genesis 14. This may indicate that Hosea may not have had the book of Genesis and relied on a tradition that differed from it. Verse 12:5 contains a similar problem.

Ashkenazi Jews have the custom of reading 11:7 through 12:12 as the haphtarah to the biblical portion Vayishlach.[1]

1. **"When Israel was a child, I loved him, and called my son out of Egypt.**

Hosea continues the theme in the prior chapter that God aided the people of Israel in the past, but the nation abandoned God. While the final passage of chapter 10 speaks about the morning of the king, this verse talks about the morning of Israel, as Hosea does in 2:17. Hosea calls Israel God's son, as in Exodus 4:22 when the deity sent Moses to Pharaoh to release the Israelites

---

1. A haphtarah is a reading from the Prophets that follows the weekly Torah reading in the Sabbath services.

from slavery. McKeating points out that in Canaanite texts the high god, El, is the father of gods and is commonly called "father of men."

2. **As they called them, so they went from them: they sacrificed to Baalim, and burned incense to graven images.**

Hosea reminds his audience, as in the prior chapter and in 2:15, 4:7, and elsewhere, that almost immediately after being saved from slavery by God, the Israelites ignored their leaders and worshipped idols (Radak).

3. **I taught Ephraim also to walk, taking them by their arms; but they knew not that I healed them.**

Like a parent, God figuratively taught Israel how to walk and how to behave. But like an indifferent and unruly child, the nation did not realize that it was God who was aiding them, or as Rashi states, they knew but acted as if they did not know. "Taking them by their arms" refers to Moses in Numbers 11:12, who speaks of leading the people "as a nursing father carries a sucking child" (Rashi).[2]

Healing may refer to the episode of the fiery serpent, also called the brazen snake, of Numbers 21:8f, named *nechustan* in Hebrew. When the people complained about insufficient bread and water, God sent poisonous snakes to kill them. After the people acknowledged their wrongdoing, God instructed Moses to make a brass serpent and place it among the people so that Israelites who looked at it would not die from their snakebites.[3]

Leaving aside the miraculous nature of the event, it is possible that looking at the *nechustan* showed that the people who did so relied on divine help.

---

2. Compare Jeremiah 31:20, "Is Ephraim a darling son to me?"

3. The text as usual is obscure, and "healing" may be a figurative way of saying that God had helped the nation by taking them out of Egypt.

Justin Martyr, the second-century Christian apologist, wrote that both the staff that Moses held during the battle with Amalek and the copper serpent on the pole were mere signs, and anyone who thought otherwise was foolish. But unlike the rabbis who saw these items as symbols designed to reorient the Israelites towards Torah observance, Justin asserted that they symbolically suggested the image of Jesus on the cross. He also commented that the military leader of the victorious battle against Amalek was named Jesus/Joshua (Dialogue with Trypho 112:2).

However, a thousand years later, many Judeans worshipped the fiery serpent and King Hezekiah destroyed it.[4]

4. **I drew them with cords of man, with bands of love; and I was to them as they who take off the yoke on their jaws, and I fed them gently.**

Hosea continues describing God's help in past times by using the analogy of how a master ("man") raises his animals: he shows them how to function with kind instruments ("bands of love," "cords of man"). "Take off the yoke" and "fed them gently" may be depicting the manner in which the master develops an obedient attitude in the animal, or it may refer to the care, food, and drink that God made available to the nation in the desert after they left Egypt.

5. **He will not return to the land of Egypt, but the Assyrian will be his king, because they refused to return.**

Rather than relying on God who had helped them in the past, the people sought aid from Egypt and Assyria, but Hosea assures his people that these nations will not help them.[5] He highlights this by repeating the idea of returning to Egypt and being ruled by Assyria, which was mentioned several times in former chapters. Israel will not return to Egypt, and will not secure their aid, but the nation will be scattered during their exile, and lose its independence to Assyria.[6]

6. **And the sword will fall on his cities, and will consume his bars, and devour them, because of their own counsels.**

Since Israel relied on its own tactics and strategies and failed to heed the prophet, there will be war. "Bars" (*badav*) are the nobles, princes, and advisors whose function is to uphold the nation. The word reappears in Jeremiah 50:36, where it is translated "boasters": "A sword is upon the boasters."

7. **And my people are wavering about returning to me; although they are called upwards, none at all will lift himself up.**

---

4. II Kings 18:4. The Christian homiletical version of the tale is in John 3:1–15.
5. II Kings 17:4ff.
6. Compare 8:13.

Although prophets urge the people to return to God, to look upward rather than down to their misguided mundane affairs, they waver and do not return.

8. **How can I give you up, Ephraim? How can I surrender you, Israel? How can I make you as Admah? How can I set you as Zeboim? My heart is turned within me; my compassions are kindled together.**

God's love for Israel, expressed in verses 1 and 4, is dramatically repeated in different words in the next four verses. God does not want Israel to suffer the same fate as Admah and Zeboim, cities of the plain that God destroyed along with Sodom and Gomorrah.[7]

Olam Hatanakh wonders why Admah and Zeboim are cited, but not Sodom and Gomorrah, and suggests that Hosea may not have had the book of Genesis and relied on a tradition that differed from it.

9. **I will not execute the fierceness of my anger. I will not return to destroy Ephraim. For I am God, and not man, the Holy One in your midst; and I will not enter the city.**

God is pictured again as loving and merciful, and the divine love and mercy far exceeds and is totally unlike that of humans. The Targum adds: "Thus, I decreed that my holy Shekhina will be among you and I will never exchange Jerusalem for another city."[8]

Hosea may be saying, as in Numbers 23:19–20, that the deity is not like humans who change their minds; if Israel returns to God, God will not destroy the capital Shomron (Kil). See the essay "The Nonbiblical Notion of Holiness" later in this book.

10. **They will walk after the Lord who will roar like a lion; for he will roar; then the children will [come] trembling from the west.**

Despite his laments and dire predictions, Hosea expects that Israel will return, rushing and trembling, to the loving God, when God calls ("roars") to them like a mother lion summoning its young, or, as stated by Kil, so that even distant Israelites will be able to hear and will return while the enemy will be

---

7. See Genesis 14, which describes the destruction of Sodom and Gomorrah, and Deuteronomy 29:22 where the two cities are named.

8. See the commentary to 5:6 regarding the meaning of Shekhina.

frightened by the ferocious roar. The word translated here as "from the west" is *mi'yam*, as ibn Ezra sees it, but others select "from the islands in the sea" or just "sea" (Olam Hatanakh).

11. **They will [come] trembling as a bird out of Egypt, and as a dove out of the land of Assyria; and I will return them to their houses," says the Lord.**

The prophet repeats what he stated previously with the much milder metaphor of the dove, also mentioned in 7:11. A symbol of peace, the dove characteristically returns to its nest.

Hosea ends his talk here with "says the Lord," as in 2:15, 18, and 23.

Chapter 12

Hosea recalls again the early divine love for Israel and the many aids given to the people. Judah is mentioned in the chapter and it is unclear whether the prophet is berating or praising the nation, and whether these remarks were in the original Hosea text.[1] He refers to the episode of Jacob's wrestling, related in Genesis 32:25. While Genesis does not disclose the identity of Jacob's wrestler, and indeed Maimonides claims that the episode was only a vision, Hosea states that Jacob's assailant was an angel. The prophet also includes additional details that are not stated in Genesis. This caused some critics to ask whether Hosea knew about the biblical book of Genesis and whether he only relied on a tradition that differs from it. This situation is similar to 11:8, where the prophet refers to Admah and Zeboim but not Sodom and Gomorrah, the two cities mentioned as being destroyed in Genesis 14.

Verse 5 is significant because it appears to confirm that the temple in Beth-el was dedicated to God, and was not a site of idol worship, and seems to indicate that Hosea felt that God intended the area of Shiloh and Beth-el as the capital of the nation and its spiritual center.

Hosea 12:13–14:10 is the haphtarah to the biblical portion Vayeitzei. The verses in Vayeitzei speak of Jacob leaving his home, while Hosea talks of returning.

1. "Ephraim compasses me about with lies, and the house of Israel with deceit; but Judah still rules with God, and is faithful with the holy ones.

---

1. See the introduction, which suggests that the mentions of Judah were late interpolations.

Many commentators place this verse as the concluding verse of the prior chapter (McKeating). The Targum, Rashi, Kara, Radak, Kil, and others construe the description of Judah as I did, in a favorable manner, but Lehrman treats the passage as a disparagement of Judah, "And Judah is yet wayward towards God, and towards the Holy One who is faithful." This latter translation raises the question: Why is Judah mentioned here? However, it fits with verse 3's mention of the Lord's "controversy with Judah." If we understand the description of Judah to be favorable, the mention of Judah is logical: Israel's deceit and abandonment appears more despicable when compared with the faithfulness of Judah. Ehrlich "corrects" some words and suggests the reading: "but Judah roams [in search of a deity], yet has God, even the most holy, who has proved true [to him]."

Olam Hatanakh notes that *kedoshim* is plural, so if it describes God, the plural emphasizes that the divine holiness far exceeds any other kind of holiness. The word *rad*, translated here as "rules," may also mean "follows [the divine way]."[2]

2. **Ephraim strives after wind, and follows the east wind; all day he multiplies lies and desolation; and they make a covenant with Assyria, and oil is carried into Egypt.**

Israel's tactic of an alliance with either Egypt or Assyria is disastrous. The idiom of striving after wind is found in Ecclesiastes 1:14 and denotes a worthless endeavor; he who runs after wind will gain nothing. The east wind is worse as it is more powerful and offers nothing positive; it is the hot sirocco that destroys vegetation.

The "oil" is olive oil, one of the chief exports of the land of Israel.

3. **The Lord has also a controversy with Judah, and will punish Jacob according to his ways; he will return to him according to his behaviors.**

Depending on how verse 1 is translated, Hosea may be stating that Judah was faithful to God at first and later abandoned God, as did Israel. Either way, the mention of Jacob appears to imply that both kingdoms that descended from Jacob will be punished. Some commentators suggest that "Judah" should

2. See the commentary on verse 5 regarding the plural indicating excess.

read "Israel" because Hosea is not addressing the southern kingdom of Judah (Olam Hatanakh).

4. **He took his brother by the heel in the womb, and with strength he strove with Elohim.**

The episode of Jacob struggling with "Elohim," a noun that is not defined in Genesis, but which Hosea uses in the next passage, is described in Genesis 32:25ff.

The prophet may be alluding to God helping Jacob from his birth. Jacob wanted to be the firstborn, as seen by his holding of Esau's heel, and he secured this right in Genesis 25:29–34 when he purchased it from his older brother. Similarly, God aided Jacob when he struggled with Elohim. But despite this assistance, Jacob – meaning Ephraim or both kingdoms – abandoned God. If the Israelites, or both kingdoms, would recall how God gave Jacob power, they would realize that they should not turn to other nations for help.[3]

While I treated the references to the patriarch Jacob positively throughout this chapter, as an example of God aiding a person, the chapter could also be read as Hosea castigating Jacob for past behavior, as he castigates Israel. In this reading, the fact that Jacob held on to Esau's heal to prevent him from emerging as the firstborn represents an attempt to thwart God/nature's plan.[4]

McKeating reads the passages negatively. Hosea "does not regard Jacob as a hero at all, and episodes which in Genesis are taken as redounding to Jacob's glory are treated by Hosea with scorn. … Hosea's interpretation surprises us only because we are more familiar with the Genesis presentation of the traditions and therefore regard it as normative." In essence, McKeating believes that Hosea had no knowledge of the Five Books of Moses, but had a tradition, written or oral, about Jacob, and his evaluation of the patriarch was negative: Jacob was evil even in the womb; he subsequently stole Esau's firstborn right, and later his blessing, and cheated his father-in-law Laban – even as the rich Israelites mistreated the poor.

---

3. This verse, indeed the entire section mentioning Jacob, is obscure. Jacob can refer to Ephraim alone, or to the two kingdoms, both descendant from Jacob. Jacob could be a reminder that God is involved in human affairs and, as an example, helped Jacob. Conversely, as indicated in the next paragraph, Hosea may be viewing Jacob negatively.

4. Genesis 25:26.

5. **So he strove with an angel and prevailed. He wept, and made supplication unto him. He found him in Beth-el, and there he would speak with us.**

Just as Jacob fearlessly fought and prevailed with divine help, so can Israel rely on God and be successful.[5]

The noun *el* means "power," and the plural Elohim denotes the "most powerful." It is used in Genesis 6:2, in the phrase "sons of Elohim," to signify "powerful men," and in Exodus 21:22 and 22:8 to describe judges. Maimonides states that the battle between Jacob and Elohim was a vision, not an actual occurrence, but our prophet sees the battle as Jacob actually striving with an angel, and making a request of him. The angel blessed him by calling him Israel, "for you strove with Elohim and with men and prevailed," implying in our prophet's mind that Jacob's descendants will receive aid from God.[6]

Rashi, who believed that angels exist and interact with humans, contends that this angel was the appointee over Esau and fought Jacob because Jacob had absconded with the blessing from their father Isaac.[7]

Hosea states "he wept" but does not identify who wept – Jacob or the angel. Rashi and Kara write that the angel wept. When the story is told in Genesis 32:23–33, there is no mention of anyone weeping. Also, in Genesis Jacob's battle did not occur in Beth-el, as Hosea says, but at the Wadi Jabbok. It is therefore possible, as mentioned above, that Hosea had a different tradition than the one in Genesis.

Alternatively, the prophet may be referring to two encounters. Beth-el may be the place where Jacob had a dream of angels going up and down a ladder. He made a vow there with conditions, and said that if the conditions are met "then the Lord will be my God." Jacob set up a pillar there and declared the

---

5. Genesis 32:27.
6. While Hosea imagines that the battle is between Jacob and an angel, the noun Elohim, as I mentioned, may simply mean a very powerful man. Thus, Hosea is either repeating a tradition he had or inventing the notion that the man with whom Jacob struggled was an angel. We should note that the man with whom Jacob wrestled said, "You strove with Elohim and with men and prevailed," including the plural "men" with Elohim. Thus, Jacob's antagonist may be saying that Jacob strove with God (in Genesis 28) and with men, referring to Esau, Laban, and himself.
7. Rashi's comment appears on Genesis 32:4, which states that Jacob send *malakhim* to Esau. The word *malakhim* could be translated as "messengers" or "angels"; Rashi contends that Jacob sent angels.

place to be "God's house," the meaning of Beth-el.[8] The mention of Beth-el may also refer to chapter 35, where God appears to Jacob and tells him to go to Beth-el, dwell there, and make an altar there "unto God who appeared to you when you fled from the face of your bother," a reference to chapter 28. Hosea's statement "he wept" may be a dramatization of the struggle in Genesis: "He said, 'Let me go for the day breaks.' And he said, 'I will not let you go unless you bless me'" (Radak).

Kil proposes a possibility that the plural "speak with us" implies that when God spoke to Jacob in Beth-el he was telling Jacob about all of his descendants. The Midrash *Yalkut Shimoni* states that the plural indicates either that in the future God will reappear to Jacob in Beth-el and change his name to Israel, or that the angel who wrestled with Jacob and who was speaking to him now tells Jacob that he will be with Jacob also in Beth-el, just as he is here now (hence the plural), and "God will speak to us." Neither of these suggestions fit the plain meaning of the Hosea text or the biblical Genesis story.

There are two significant points here. (1) The phrase "there he would speak with us" seems to confirm the view expressed in this book that the people of the northern nation did not worship idols, or at least most of them did not, and that Beth-el was considered a house of God, not a place for idol worship. (2) The verse also seems to support the view I expressed in the Joshua volume of this series[9] that the Five Books of Moses intended that the Shiloh area be Israel's capital and its spiritual center. Beth-el was in this area.

In regard to the first point, the plural use of "us" bothered many commentators, such as Ehrlich, who did not want to see Beth-el as a site of divine worship, so they contended that the plural should be reduced to the singular, the usage in the Septuagint and Peshitta.

6. **Even the Lord, the God of hosts; the Lord [*y-h-v-h*] is his name.**

This verse has no meaning unless we understand that "God of hosts" denotes that God controls everything and that "name" in the Bible, beside indicating nomenclature, also signifies essence. Hosea is telling Israel/Jacob that they should rely on God because God controls everything and the divine essence

---

8. Genesis 28:10–22.
9. Pages 79–83.

is *y-h-v-h*, "I will be what I will be" – I am what I want to be and all will be what I want it to be.

7. **Therefore, return to your God, keep mercy and judgment, and wait on your God continually.**

Hosea tells the people that since God controls all and is all-powerful, they should cease forsaking God and return to God. God wants mercy and judgment, not sacrifices, as stated in 6:6, 10:12, Micah 6:8, Maimonides's *Guide* 3:32, and many other places.

8. **As a Canaanite, the balances of deceit are in his hand; he loves to oppress.**

Israel/Jacob does not engage in mercy and judgment, but acts with self-interest and deceit. The term Canaanite in Hebrew denotes the nation, the country, and a merchant.[10] The "balances of deceit" are reminiscent of the scales that crooked merchants manipulate to their benefit.

9. **Ephraim said, 'Surely I have become rich. I have found wealth. No wrong-doing can be found in all my works.'**

These are words that the prophet imagines Ephraim saying to justify itself. Human nature tends to ascribe wisdom and good deeds to the rich, or at least Ephraim is doing so here. Alternatively, the rich are claiming that if all their activities were investigated, it would be discovered that they acquired their wealth justly and not by taking advantage of the poor.

Rashi and Kara presume that this passage is pointing us to a legend concerning the brothers. The Bible relates that when Joseph's silver cup was found in Benjamin's sack, Joseph threatened to take Benjamin as a slave. The legend adds that Jeroboam I found a contract between Joseph and his brothers that coerced the brothers to become Joseph's slaves in place of Benjamin. Jeroboam therefore said: "All Israelites are slaves to me since I am a descendant of Joseph, and all that these slaves have belongs to me. Thus I can do with them as I like and 'no wrongdoing can be found in my works.'"

---

10. For example, Rashi defines Canaanite in Genesis 38:2 as "merchant," so that we should not think that Judah married the daughter of a Canaanite.

10. **But I am the Lord your God from the land of Egypt. I will make you return to tents, as in the days of the appointed season.**

The rich may fool other humans, but not God who is all-powerful and all-knowing. God knows that the rich engaged in deceit and will punish them. Just as God saved the Israelites from slavery, God can also do the opposite. The "appointed season" (*yemei moed*) may refer to Succoth, mentioned also in 9:5, when Israel dwells in tents as part of the observance of the holiday. At that time God can make the tent dwelling festive and enjoyable, or turn the time into exile when the people who are driven from their homes will at best find shelter in tents. Some commentators theorize that this verse is describing the nation wandering homeless, as in the forty-year desert experience in the days of Moses (Olam Hatanakh). Rashi adds that the people will use the time in the tents to study Torah. The Targum, New English Bible, and Jewish Publication Society translate *moed* as "in the days of old."

Ehrlich understands "I will make you return to tents, as in the days of the appointed season" as a reference to the holiday of Succoth, at the end of the harvest, when so many Israelites traveled to Jerusalem to worship at the temple. There was not sufficient housing for them all, and many had to sleep in tents. He contends that this is the origin of using succoth (huts) during the holiday of Succoth, and the holiday that had at first been called *hachag*, "the holiday," was later named after these huts.

11. **I spoke to prophets, and I multiplied visions, and used similitudes by the ministry of the prophets.**

What God desires from the people is not hidden. God frequently instructed the prophets to teach the divine lessons, and they did so in easy-to-understand parables, such as the tale of Hosea and Gomer in this book, and as stated in Numbers 12:6.

12. **Yes, Gilead gives itself to iniquity, they have become very vain; in Gilgal they sacrifice bullocks, their altars will be as heaps in the furrows of the fields.**

Hosea speaks of Gilead in 5:1 and 6:8, and of Gilgal in 4:15 and 9:15. Again, the wrongdoing here may be that the altars were for idols, as the Targum consistently contends, or that sacrifices were offered to God without showing mercy and justice to fellow humans. Ehrlich translates that the altars were as numerous as the "droppings of dung" by animals in the furrows they had ploughed. Kil notes that it was in Gilead that Jacob made a treaty with his father-in-law Laban and kept it; in contrast, his descendants broke their covenant with God.[11]

13. Jacob fled into the field of Aram, and Israel served for a wife, and for a wife he kept sheep.

Hosea returns to verses 3–5 to remind his people of Jacob: when Jacob faced the ire of his brother Esau who sought to kill him, he fled to Aram and used the opportunity, prompted by his mother's advice, to find a wife. He fell in love with Rachel and worked to gain her as a wife.[12] The prophet implies that God aided Jacob in gaining wives and wealth, so it is inappropriate for Ephraim to claim in verse 9 that the nation obtained wealth by its own labors. However, Ehrlich sees this passage as continuing the negative portrayal of Jacob: he had to run from home after cheating his brother Esau out of the blessing and he had to work as a near slave to acquire his wives, which was an inappropriate degradation as other people did not act in this way.

14. And by a prophet the Lord brought Israel out of Egypt, and by a prophet was he preserved.

Hosea returns to the thoughts of verse 11 and reminds his people that God delivered Israel from slavery and cared for them in the desert through the prophet Moses. The rescue was not accomplished by human effort. Why, he implies, do you not listen to a prophet now?

15. Ephraim provoked him to anger most bitterly; therefore, his blood will be cast upon him, and his Lord will return his reproach unto him."

But the people refused to listen, which metaphorically provoked God's anger[13] with a disastrous result. The people's blood will be on their own hands, and since they do not return to God, God will ironically return to punish them.

---

11. Genesis 31:22–54.
12. Genesis 29ff.
13. Maimonides taught in his *Guide* that God does not act like humans and has no human emotions, He explains that though the Torah states that God becomes angry and will execute punishment, it does so only in order to encourage the people to behave.

Chapter 13

As is his habit, Hosea revisits ideas using different metaphoric images. He talks again about the early years of the nation – God aided Israel, the people prospered and abandoned God, they clamored for a king to help them rather than relying on God, they caused God anguish, and they will be punished. The mood of the chapter, as in most of the book, is agony and disappointment.

1. **"When Ephraim spoke, there was trembling, he exalted himself in Israel; but when he offended in Baal, he died.**

   Continuing his focus on the early years of his people, before the nation divided under kings Jeroboam I and Rehoboam, Hosea states that Ephraim was originally strong and fearful, causing other nations to tremble. *Nasa*, translated here as "exalted himself," could also be understood as "prince": Ephraim was the prince of the tribes (Rashi).[1] However, these were days when the nation followed the divine way. When it went astray from God and relied on its own strength, it showed its weakness, as if it were dead. Verse 7:9 is somewhat similar.

   It is unclear what the prophet's mention of Baal refers to. Possibilities include: (1) Hosea is repeating his description of the nation worshiping Baal-peor during the days of Moses, as in 9:10; (2) Hosea is referring to the

---

1. The center of worship during the days of the judges was Shiloh, which was in the territory of Ephraim. Samuel was the last leader from this tribe until the establishment of the monarchy under King Saul. This lasted a long time, by some estimates over four hundred years. Jeroboam I reestablished Ephraim hegemony, with the Shiloh area having a temple again in Beth-el.

worship of idols during the dynasties of King Ahab and King Jehoahaz. I Kings 16:31–33, among other passages, speaks about the worship of Baal in the days of Ahab,[2] and II Kings 13:6 states that during the time of Jehoahaz the Asherah remained;[3] (3) the passage refers to Jeroboam I, who rebelled against the house of David and established the kingdom of Israel to the north of Judah (Rashi and Kara); (4) Hosea is describing the conditions of his own time. See commentary to 8:4. However, in view of the wording of the next verse, "and now they continue to do wrong more and more," it seems clear that verse 1 is describing the past. While the people are acting improperly during the lifetime of Hosea, they are not worshipping idols. See the essay about the golden calf later in this book.

2. **And now they continue to do wrong more and more, and have made for themselves molten images of their silver, and images according to their own understanding, all of them the work of craftsmen. They say of them, 'Let the men that sacrifice kiss the calves.'**

Concluding his reminiscing of Israel's history, Hosea turns to his own generation and criticizes his people for making images, but not idols, as discussed in the commentary to 8:4. He uses the polemic of 8:6. The word for "wrong" is *cheit*, "missing the mark," discussed in the essay on sin later in this book. The words for "the men that sacrifice" is *zovchei adam*, which literally is "those who sacrifice men"; this cannot be what Hosea intends because there is no history in Israel of sacrificing men. In is unclear who are "they" and "them." "They" may be those who use the fetishes and "them" may be the fetishes. Alternatively, "they" could be the more intelligent in the population who mock the people who use and even kiss the fetishes, like Jews kissing a mezuzah, and Christians a cross. They ridicule them and say, "Why only kiss the inanimate symbols? Why not go a step further and kiss live calves!" The Targum states that "they" are the false prophets who lead the people astray. The Targum, Rashi, Kara, Radak, and others contend that the passage is saying that the generation of Jeroboam II worships idols.

2. Ahab's son Jehoram (Joram) "put away the pillars of Baal that his father had made" (II Kings 3:2) and his successor Jehu "destroyed Baal out of Israel" (II Kings 10:28).
3. The Canaanites believed that Asherah (also called Astarte) was the wife of Baal.

3. **Therefore, they will be as the morning cloud, and as the dew that passes away early, as the chaff that is driven with the wind out of the threshing floor, and as the smoke out of the chimney.**

As a result of their ridiculous focus on fetishes rather than treating their neighbors kindly, the population will disappear quickly as a morning cloud, as dew, as chaff in the wind, and as smoke, repeating what was said in 6:4 and other passages.

4. **Yet I am the Lord your God from the land of Egypt, and you will know no God but me, and beside me there is no savior.**

These images will not help the nation; kissing them will bring no aid, and never has done so. The people must rely on God, who has demonstrated divine aid. God helped the people most significantly in the time of the exodus from Egypt – as stated in 12:14 and elsewhere, and as will be recalled in detail in some of the following verses.

This verse mentions two, but only two, of the commands in the Decalogue. See the introduction to chapter 4 where the question is raised whether Hosea knew about the Torah in general and the Decalogue in particular.

5. **I knew you in the wilderness, in the land of great drought.**

Among many other aids, God gave the people water in an area that has little water. The term "know," as mentioned previously, indicates a close relationship and is even used to describe sex, as discussed in the commentary to 4:2. Hosea frequently refers to the people "not knowing" God to indicate their abandonment of God.

6. **When they were fed, they became satisfied, and when they were satisfied, their heart was exalted, and then they forgot me.**

Hosea is reflecting basic psychology: many people turn to God only when they feel the need for help. The nation forgot God soon after leaving the desert and entering Canaan, repeating the image in 4:10.

I translated *s-v-a* as "satisfied," rather than "full," following Maimonides's advice to leave the dinner table before one is full, as even modern doctors teach: it takes about twenty minutes for the body to register that it is full, and if one leaves the table feeling full, he or she has overeaten.

7. **Therefore, I will be to them as a lion, as a leopard I observe them by the way.**

    God will cease helping Israel and will turn on them through vicious invading nations who are like ferocious beasts, echoing the image of 5:14, which is restated in the next passage using another metaphor.

    Bothered by the anthropomorphic image of God acting like an animal, the Targum substitutes *memra*, God's "command" or "wisdom," in verses 7, 8, 9, 14, and 15.

8. **I will meet them as a bear that is bereaved of her whelps, and will rend their closed hearts, and there I will devour them like a lion; the wild beast will tear them.**

    Hosea intensifies his threat by speaking about an enraged bereaved bear and a devouring lion; both will tear Israel's divided heart apart, as predicted in 10:2. The heart in ancient times was considered the seat of the intellect. The rending of the heart is therefore appropriate, for the people did not use their intelligence well, as stated in 4:6.

9. **Israel, you destroyed yourself; you are against me, against your help.**

    The Israelites' blood is on their own hands, as affirmed in 4:2 and 12:15.

10. **I will be your king now and will save you in all your cities, as well as your judges, to whom you said, 'Give me a king and princes.'**

    The prophet is expressing the divine anger over the Israelites' rejection of divine help and their desire for a king, as implied in 9:9 and described in I Samuel 8:5.

11. **I gave you a king despite my anger, and took him away in my wrath.**

    Again, the image is unclear. Hosea may be continuing his interpretation of I Samuel 8:5 when the people approached the prophet Samuel, the last of more than a dozen judges, and demanded a king to help them as kings help other nations. In response, God tells Samuel that he should not feel rebuffed; it is God who is being snubbed. God then commands Samuel to make Saul the first king of Israel, but later eliminated him and his son Jonathan because Saul did not carry out the divine order to destroy all of Amalek.

Alternatively, our prophet may be referring to the kingship of Jeroboam I: while God allowed Jeroboam I to abandon the monarchy of the house of David, God later destroyed the reign of his son.

12. The iniquity of Ephraim is bound up; his misbehavior is laid up in store.

Hosea repeats the same thought in different words: God knows what Ephraim has been doing, has metaphorically kept a list, and will punish the nation. The Hebrew has an alliteration, each phrase beginning with a *tzadi*. The word for "iniquity" is *avon*, and for "misbehavior" *cheit*; both terms are defined in the essay on sin below.

The prophet may be alluding to the records kept by ancient kings of the acts of their vassals, as in Ezra 4:14–19, or, as ibn Ezra explains, God has their misdeeds in mind.

13. The pains of a travailing woman will come upon him. He is an unwise son. It is time that he should not stay long in the place of the breaking forth of children.

Hosea uses a new and striking metaphor in this verse. Just as a pregnant woman frequently suffers greatly during childbirth until her baby is born, Israel should realize that it is like the baby who has not yet burst forth from his mother's womb, who is causing his mother enormous pain. Israel must break out of the womb, a metaphor for becoming wise and treating people appropriately, so that the nation (mother) and its citizens (son) can live in peace under the guidance of divine law.

14. Should I ransom them from the power of the grave? Should I redeem them from death? Death will be plagues! Grave will be destruction! Pity will be hidden from my eyes!

Hosea pictures God's lament: Should I send this people to the grave? If God forsakes Israel as Israel discarded God, the people will not only die, but they will suffer greatly and the divine attribute of mercy will be annulled.

15. For though he be fruitful like his brethren, an east wind will come, the wind of the Lord will rise from the wilderness, and his spring will become dry, and his fountain dried up, he will spoil the treasure of all pleasant vessels."

The prophet reuses the metaphors of "wind," found in 4:19, 8:7, 12:2, and 13:3;

"wilderness," from 2:5, 2:16, 9:10, and 13:5; and "east wind," from 12:2. He also repeats the word *yaphri*, "be fruitful," as an ironic play on the name Ephraim, as in 14:9. The use of "east wind" here may be a stand-in for Assyria, which was to the east of Israel, or it may simply allude to the damaging effect of the turbulent east wind.

Chapter 14

Chapter 14 is significant because of the interpretation the rabbis gave to verse 2, according to which Hosea introduced the concept of "repentance"; for an analysis of this topic see the essay on repentance later in this book. Some scholars accept this view and say that repentance is so uncharacteristic of our prophet that it is clear to them that verses 2–10 were originally not part of Hosea (Interpreter's Bible).[1] Also significant is the book's final verse, which summarizes the message of the book.

The haphtarah for Shabbat Shuva, the Sabbath between the holidays of Rosh Hashanah and Yom Kippur, is Hosea 14:2–10 and Micah 7:18–20.

1. **"Samaria will become desolate; for she rebelled against her God. They will fall by the sword. Their infants will be dashed in pieces, and their pregnant women will be ripped up.**

   Many scholars, such as Ehrlich, are convinced that this verse belongs as the concluding passage of the prior chapter because it continues the thought in 13:15.

   The image of the horrors committed against a pregnant woman is also in 13:13. Rather than portraying the Israelites being so disrespectful of God, the Targum softens the critique to rebelling against God's *memra*, the "word" or "command" of the Lord. "*Memra*" is also inserted in verse 6 and twice in 9.

---

1. This judgment is based on the erroneous view that Hosea felt that his mission was to stop idol worship, a view that also prompted some scholars to suggest that certain verses need to be changed, such as 12:5.

2. **Return, Israel, unto the Lord your God; for you have stumbled in your iniquity.**

    The word used for iniquity is *avon* here and in verse 3. See the essay on sin.

    Jewish tradition sees Hosea speaking about "repentance" in this verse and accordingly arranged that this prophetic lesson should be read as the haphtarah for the Shabbat between the holidays of Rosh Hashanah and Yom Kippur, which the rabbis called Shabbat Shuva, the Sabbath of Repentance. However, this rabbinical enactment is a homily, as explained in the essay on repentance later in this book. Hosea is not speaking about "repentance," a concept that did not exist during his age. He was reasserting his oft-repeated theme: You abandoned God as an adulterous woman left her husband. God, as her husband, still loves her, and wants her to "return."

    Deuteronomy 30:2 is similar to 14:2, "return to the Lord your God and listen to his voice," and Jewish commentators recognize that Deuteronomy is not speaking about repentance. Hosea is reiterating 2:9, which has Gomer saying, "I will go back to my first husband, for then I was better off than now." He is reflecting the teaching of the later prophet Jeremiah: "Return, you backsliding children, I will heal your backsliding."[2] Hosea mentions "healing" in verse 5.

    McKeating suggests that while at present "stumble" in modern English describes a person "thrown momentarily off balance, of a near-mishap. But in Hebrew it is a much stronger word. 'To stumble' in the Bible means 'to come to utter disaster.'"

    While the texts explicitly states "Israel" and many scholars insist that Hosea is only addressing the northern kingdom, Rashi writes that God is addressing Judah here and saying: "You should see what I did to Israel and return to God so as not suffer the same punishment."

3. **Take with you words, and return to the Lord. Say to him, 'Take away all iniquity, and accept what is good, so will we render for calves [the offerings] of our lips.**

    The prophet advises his people again, as in 3:5, to tell God by means of actions that they will "take away all iniquity" – they will cease acting improperly with

    _____

    2. Jeremiah 3:22.

others, but will treat them with mercy and justice ("what is good"). They will realize, as Hosea stated in 6:6, that God is not satisfied with sacrifices, and instead they will offer kind words and proper treatment of their fellows. Rather than actions, as stated above, the Targum interprets "words" as confessions. But, actually, Hosea is reflecting 6:6 and the words of I Samuel 15:22, "Behold, to obey is better than sacrifice, and to listen than the fat of rams."

4. **Assyria will not save us; we will not ride on horses; neither will we call any more the work of our hands "our gods," for it is in you that the fatherless find mercy.'**

This is part of what Israel should say/realize: They now know that Assyria will not help them, and they will not use the horses from Egypt, cited in 1:7 and 2:20. They will reject their fetishes and recognize God, their father.

I will heal their returning. I will love them freely, for my anger is returned away from him.

5. **"I will heal their returning" should be understood as "I will heal those who return" and will forget their misdeeds (Rashi, Kara, Altschuler, and others).**

Twice using a form of *shuv*, "return," God declares that the divine action will be reciprocal: Israel will return and the divine anger previously expressed will cease (return). The remaining passages of this book foresee a happy future for Israel if they return to God.

Hosea also repeats the metaphor "heal," as in 5:13, 6:1, and 7:1, seeing the Israelite behavior as a disease.

6. **I will be as the dew unto Israel: he will grow as the lily, and cast forth his roots as Lebanon.**

While "dew" described the hasty destruction of Israel in 6:4 and 13:3, the prophet uses it now in connection with the restoration of the bounty of Israel. "Lily" symbolizes fragrance and, hence, good health and enjoyment, and "Lebanon," as indicated in the next verse, represents a land of plenty.

Lebanon is mentioned three times in this chapter and a total of seventy-one times throughout the Hebrew Bible. Verses such as Deuteronomy 1:7,

3:25, 11:24, and Joshua 1:4 seem to indicate that the ancient Israelites felt that Lebanon was a very fruitful land and an area that belonged to them.

The prophet mentions Lebanon here because its trees have long roots that hold the trees firmly (Rashi).

7. **His branches will spread, and his beauty will be as the olive tree, and his fragrance as Lebanon.**

The prophet now uses still other descriptive metaphors for Israel's future prosperity if the nation returns to God.

8. **They who dwell under his shadow will return; they will revive [as] corn, and grow as the vine; their fragrance will be as the wine of Lebanon.**

Israel in the future, after they return, will revive in huge numbers as corn at the time of harvest. They will increase as spreading vines, and will be as gratifying to one another and to God as the tasty wines of Lebanon.

The Targum inserts into verse 8 that in the future the dead will be resurrected and into verse 10 that the wicked will be delivered to Gehinnom (hell) because they did not walk in the ways of the Lord.

9. **Ephraim [shall say]: 'What have I to do anymore with images?' [God states:] 'I respond and observe him.' [Then Ephraim says:] 'I am like a leafy cypress tree. Your fruit is found from me.'**

This verse is most likely a dialogue between Ephraim and God. Finally obeying Hosea, Ephraim speaks, as directed in verse 3, and admits that it has no need for images. God responds by assuring the nation that it will enjoy prosperity, as in verses 5–8. Then the nation realizes it will be prosperous ("like a leafy cypress tree"), with bounty given by God ("Your fruit is found from me").

10. **Whoever is wise will understand these things, will be prudent and know them, that the ways of the Lord are right, that they just walk in them, while transgressors stumble in them.**

"Transgressors," *poshim*, translates literally as "rebels," as explained in the essay on sin. Hosea ends his book as he began. As Hosea's wife abandoned him, so did Israel rebel against God. Both the prophet and God seek the return of the rebels. The word "return" is stressed, appearing five times in this final chapter.[3]

The prophet envisions that both just people and transgressors walk in the ways of the Lord, but although both seek to serve God, the transgressors stumble. It appears that Hosea is referring back to 6:6 – true, the people of Israel are not worshipping idols and are piously offering their sacrifices to the Lord, but this is not what God desires; God wants the people to act properly with one another.[4]

McKeating suggests: "This closing verse was added by some Jewish scribe long after Hosea's time. It sums up what the scribe took to be the moral of the book." The Interpreter's Bible and others agree.

Whether written by the prophet himself or by others, Hosea's concluding summary seems to confirm that the prophet is not castigating his countrymen for idol worship, but for their failures in moral conduct. The prophet does not mention idol worship in his summary, but speaks of the "ways of the Lord" – this does not suggest idol worship, for God is not involved in worship. The wording fits with the understanding that Hosea wants his people to act with mercy, graciousness, abundance of goodness, truth, and justice with all people – the attributes of God listed in Exodus 33:6–7. This is *imitatio dei*, the teaching that one should imitate divine behavior. The rabbis saw this teaching in Leviticus 19:2, "Be holy because I the Lord am holy."[5]

This gives more meaning to the Gomer parable in the first three chapters of Hosea. It was not the abandonment that bothered the prophet so much as the immorality of her behavior, her mistreatment of the person who deserved consideration, her lack of compassion and concern.

---

3. Verses 2, 3, 5 (twice), and 8.

4. We are reminded of Maimonides's famous parable of the palace (*Guide of the Perplexed* 3:51), in which he describes various kinds of people who try to enter the palace to come close to God. He states that "those who arrive at the palace, but [are unable to enter it and instead] go roundabout it, are those who devote themselves exclusively to the study of practical law; they believe traditionally in true principles of faith, and learn the practical worship of God," but do not devote themselves to philosophy, to the study of laws of nature, to "*hesed* (loving-kindness), *mishpat* (judgment), and *zedakah* (righteousness)" – principles that Maimonides discusses in *Guide* 3:53. These pious people just wander about outside of the palace. Translation by M. Friedlander (New York: Dover, 1881).

5. Babylonian Talmud, *Sota* 14a and *Shabbat* 133b.

Essays

Midrashic Interpretations of Hosea

In his "Introduction to Perek Chelek," Maimonides wrote that a person who reads a Midrash and believes that what is written is true is a fool, and one who dismisses it entirely since it is not true is also a fool. The proper way to understand Midrashim is to realize that they were composed as parables that teach lessons.

BABYLONIAN TALMUD

The Babylonian Talmud, *Pesachim* 87a, states that Jeroboam II ruled for forty-one years as a reward because he did not accept the slander that the priest Amaziah said about the prophet Amos in Amos 7:10–11. It also states that Hosea was a contemporary of Amos, Micah, and Isaiah, but was greater than they because he was the first prophet to teach the importance of *teshuva*, "repentance," in 14:2.[1] *Pirkei d'Rabbi Eliezer* adds that Hosea also taught Israel how to pray.[2]

Pesachim also states that the opening phrase of Hosea 1:2, "When the Lord began to speak with Hosea," indicates that Hosea prophesied before Amos, Micah, and Isaiah. Rashi and Kara acknowledge that the simple meaning of the verse is that this was the beginning of Hosea's prophecies. Many scholars differ with the rabbis and contend that Amos preceded Hosea.

Pesachim's view is that Hosea actually married a prostitute.[3] "Then [God] said, I will order him: 'Send her away from thy presence.' If he is able to send [her]

---

1. Curiously, the Talmud does not mention Jonah, who prophesied to Jeroboam II that God advised him to expand his kingdom.
2. *Pirkei d'Rabbi Eliezer* 44:23.
3. The wording is "take a harlot." The Bible does not use the term "marry" anywhere; it is always "take." The Talmud does use the term "marriage" many times elsewhere, but not here.

away, so will I send Israel away."[4] Hosea, according to the Talmud, did not want to send her away. Whereupon, God said, "I will also not send Israel away." One opinion in the Talmud defines Gomer's name as "complete," meaning that she satisfied the lust of many men. Another said it denotes that Assyria will destroy Israel during Gomer's lifetime.

RASHI

Commenting on the huge promises of gifts that God promises Israel if she returns to God, Rashi tells a parable: It is like a king who becomes angry at his wife and summons a scribe to write a divorce. Before the scribe arrives, the king's feelings soften and he no longer wants the divorce. When the scribe arrives and asks why he was called, the king does not want to reveal that he had thought of divorcing his queen. He therefore says, "I summoned you to write a promise to my wife that I am giving her more wealth than I previously promised."

OTHER TALMUDIC AND MIDRASHIC INTERPRETATIONS

Pirkei d'Rabbi Eliezer 33:90 contends that Hosea prophesied about Israel for ninety years. The Babylonian Talmud, *Megillah* 15a, and *Leviticus Rabba* 6:6 state that when a prophet's father's name is appended to his own, the father was also a prophet. While there is no prophecy attributed to Hosea's father Beeri in the Bible, they assign two verses in Isaiah (8:19–20) to Beeri.

Leviticus Rabba 36:6 opines that the helpful power of *zekhut avot*, "merit of the fathers," ceased during Hosea's lifetime. This concept taught that the merit that a person accumulated for his good deeds would be stored, and if the person who earned the merit did not use it, his descendants (and, according to another opinion, anyone) could draw upon the merit as one would draw money from a bank, and use the merit for his benefit.[5]

---

4. Translation from the Soncino Talmud.
5. It is possible that this Midrash gave this interpretation to explain how it was possible for Israel to be destroyed when this should not have happened.

The Ascendancy and Decline of Ephraim

Jeroboam I had a good historical claim to be the leader of Israel, although this claim is not explicit in the Bible. It started with Jacob and continued until the time of the prophet and judge Samuel.

Jacob considered his son Joseph as his firstborn. According to the interpretation of many commentators, including Rashi, Jacob gave Joseph a double portion, which was characteristically given to the firstborn.[1] When he was dying, Jacob selected Joseph's younger son Ephraim as the firstborn and said that Ephraim would become great.[2] When Moses was nearing death, God told him to select Joshua as Israel's future leader. Joshua was of the tribe of Ephraim.[3]

Joshua led the people into Canaan. After he felt the land was sufficiently conquered, he placed the Tent of Meeting in Shiloh, which was in the territory of Ephraim.[4] The Tent of Meeting, which contained the Ark, remained in the territory of Ephraim until Shiloh was destroyed by the Philistines some 300 to 350 years later, during the lifetime of Samuel.[5]

In my books on Joshua and Judges, I reported repeatedly on the conflicts

1. Genesis 48:22.
2. Genesis 48:1–21.
3. Deuteronomy 34:9.
4. Joshua 18:1; 19:51; 22:9; Psalms 78:60.
5. We have no information regarding how long a period this was and commentators offer different numbers. I Kings 6:1 states that King Solomon began to build the first temple 480 years after the exodus, which would mean that Samuel lived about 350 years after the exodus. This dating is contested by modern scholars.

between Judah and Ephraim concerning which tribe would lead Israel. When the people demanded of Samuel that he select a king,[6] Samuel selected Saul from the tribe of Benjamin,[7] perhaps hoping that since Saul was from neither Ephraim nor Judah, and since the tribe of Benjamin was situated between the two tribes, Saul would be acceptable to the two tribes.

Later, when David of the tribe of Judah became king, he, like Samuel, sought to appease Ephraim. He selected Jerusalem as the site of his kingdom and the place where the temple would be built, since Jerusalem was situated between Judah and Ephraim.[8]

In sum, it should surprise no one that the tribe of Ephraim, which enjoyed ascendancy for hundreds of years and was deprived of leadership, may have had festering anger. Thus, as soon as the tribe under the leadership of Jeroboam saw an opportunity, when King Rehoboam the grandson of King David refused to reduce their taxes, they broke away from the tribe of Judah and established their own kingdom.[9]

---

6. I Samuel 8.
7. I Samuel 9.
8. II Samuel 7.
9. I Kings 12.

The Origin of Sin

The root p-sh-a appears in 7:13, 8:1, and elsewhere. It means "rebel," not "sin." Hosea berates the people repeatedly, telling them they abandoned God and that God is displeased. God chides them either for worshipping idols or for acting immorally, but nowhere does Hosea or God say they sinned, for the concept of sin did not exist at that time. It is a Christian invention.

THE BIBLICAL CONCEPTION OF SIN

There is no concept of "sin" in the Hebrew Bible in the sense of a distorting stain upon the soul that requires a kind of supernatural atonement or cleansing process, as the concept is understood today. To the contrary, wrong behavior is seen in Scripture in a rational, natural way. The Hebrew Bible speaks of three distinct categories of wrongs. There is *cheit*, the misstep, literally meaning "missing the mark," as if one were shooting an arrow and hitting the outer rims of the target and missing the shooter's goal, its center. The Bible mentions it 34 times. The second, *pesha*, occurring 93 times, is a conscious rebellious act such as taking revenge, stealing, or murder. The third, *avon*, cited in 233 instances, is an error, an unintentional act that nevertheless has harmful consequences.

Understood in this natural way, it should be clear that the misdeed is something that shouldn't provoke passive feelings of guilt and prayerful recitations, needing clergy or a psychiatrist to erase it. Individuals should recognize what they did wrong, think why they did the wrong, take actions that remedy the consequences, and assure that there will be no repetition.[1]

---

1. This is the rational understanding of Maimonides in his *Mishneh Torah, Hilkhot Teshuva.*

THE NEW TESTAMENT AND EARLY CHRISTIANS AGREE

The New Testament describes Jesus retaining this understanding of resolving wrong behavior by physical acts. Jesus is quoted as saying in Matthew 5:17–18 that he did not come to change the law: "Do not think that I came to abolish the law or the prophets. I did not come to abolish but to fulfill. For truly I say to you, until heaven and earth shall pass away, not one dot will pass from the law until all is accomplished."[2]

Paul, who did not know Jesus and who brought his understanding of Jesus' message to non-Jews, wrote that Jesus taught that converts to Judaism must obey the Torah. He was an observant Jew. He wrote in Philippians 3:6, "As to righteousness under the law, I am blameless." In Romans 3:31, he said, "Do we nullify the law by this faith? Not at all. Rather, we uphold the law." He, like Jesus, attended the temple and he made no statement that contradicted the three-part biblical understanding of wrong behavior. Paul's main message, a message of the Torah, was to turn away from idols. Paul, who felt he must convert pagans, opposed circumcision for "gentiles-in-Christ" since he was not converting them to Judaism, but only having them accept the teachings of Jesus. But if the convert wanted to become fully Jewish – for Christianity at the time was a branch of Judaism – circumcision was necessary, as it was required of all other Jews.

The second-century Christian thinkers agreed. Valentinus (around 130) defined "sin" in his "Gospel of Truth" as "a function of ignorance," "error," a mistake. Marcion (around 140) and Justin Martyr (around 150) agreed. As Justin Martyr wrote in Trypho 141, sin is when someone does something "contrary to right reason."

ORIGINAL SIN – A NEW NOTION

When then did Christianity change? It did so with Augustine (354–430). Contrary to Jewish teachings that God is good and God's creations are good, as stated in Genesis 1, Augustine taught that people are born with the stain of sin. According to Augustine, humanity was created with an ingrained disability; left to its own devices, without God's mercy, people can only sin.

Rather than seeing the story of Adam and Eve as an allegory, as Maimonides did in his *Guide of the Perplexed* 1:2, Augustine accepted the tale as historical reality

---

2. In the Greek, the word for "dot" is "iota." It refers to the Hebrew tenth letter *yud*, which is the smallest letter in the Hebrew alphabet, just a little larger than a dot.

and gave it a new interpretation that is not explicit in the text. Adam was the originator of sin. Augustine believed that Adam, in some mystical way, contained all humanity in him. His sin, according to this mystic view, became his descendants' sin – they sinned when he sinned. After Adam, human will is defective: people function with a diminished capacity, unable to achieve the good if unassisted by divine grace. Humanity is condemned. In his *City of God* 13:23, Augustine wrote that the "inheritance of sin and death [is] conveyed to us by birth." All people of all faiths are "part of *massa damnata* [the massive damnation], justly condemned because of Adam's sin."

God, according to Augustine's new and radical view, saves only a small part of humanity, not all; Augustine does not explain why God selects some people and abandons others to hell because of Adam's sin. Augustine's god is violently and arguably irrationally angry at sin and perhaps even at God's own creations, and redeems only a small number of people, enough to show divine mercy. God is no longer the creator of what is good, but is emotional and vindictive. Yet, Augustine adds, somehow in some unknowable way, despite punishing innocent people, God is just. It seems reasonable to suppose that psychiatry is an outgrowth of the acceptance of original sin's notion that people should feel guilt and anguish when they do something they think is wrong, rather than accepting the ancient view that mistakes can be rectified by recognizing the error, deciding not to repeat it, and doing all that is reasonable to repair what was wrong, such as apologizing for an insult one made and by paying back the money stolen.

AUGUSTINE'S EFFECT ON SOCIETY

Many Christians, as well as many Jews who have absorbed Christian ideas, have forgotten the biblical concept of wrong behavior, and call Augustine's invention of "original sin" a mystery and an integral part of religion. But it is only a mystery because it is inexplicable, irrational, indeed harmful, and not part of original Judaism or Christianity.

A tragic example is the philosopher Rabbi Hasdai Crescas (c. 1340–c. 1410), who wrote a book entitled *The Refutation of the Christian Principles*.[3] He wrote the book because many Jews were murdered by Christian riots, including his only son.

---

3. SUNY Series in Jewish Philosophy. New York: State University of New York Press, 1992.

Jewish communities were destroyed and a host of Jews converted to Christianity to avoid future persecutions. As a leader of Spanish Jewry, he felt obliged to do what he could to return the converts to Judaism. Yet, without realizing what he was doing, he included the Christian idea of original sin in his *Light of the Lord*. He states that Jews were absolved of the original sin when they were circumcised. This idea about being absolved was also a Christian teaching – that prior to the appearance of Jesus circumcision saved the Jews from the impact and punishment of the original sin. Some rabbis in the Babylonian Talmud, in *Avoda Zara* 22b, *Shabbat* 145b–146a, and *Yevamot* 103b, also accepted this notion.

The Nonbiblical Notion of Holiness

The Five Books of Moses stress the importance of holiness in Leviticus 19:1ff – "You shall be holy; for I the Lord your God am holy." Yet later thinkers understood holiness in radically different ways than the Bible. The following essay explores the ways in which the concept has been discussed in Jewish thought.

THE BIBLICAL CONCEPT OF HOLINESS

The concept of "holiness," meaning that something or someone is sacred, does not exist in the Bible. Scholars say that the biblical word *kedusha*, which is usually translated today as "holiness," means "separate." When the Bible asserts that God is holy it signifies that God is totally separate and distinct from humans. When it commands Israelites to be holy, it requires that they should separate from pagan practices and act reasonably.[1]

Holiness is not an ingredient. Something that is called "holy" does not radiate or convey sanctity. A person touching a holy person or object is not elevated or changed in any way. If a holiness Geiger counter existed, and if the counter were placed next to any object or person called holy, it would not click.

TRYING TO MAKE A POINT

Calling someone or something holy should remind listeners of the queen's observation in Shakespeare's *Hamlet*: "The lady doth protest too much." The queen was

---

1. It should surprise no one that the biblical meaning of words is different than how the words are used today. *Nefesh* in the Torah, for example, is not "soul," but "person." *Emuna* is not "faith," but "steadfastness."

saying: the lady who protested was too gushy and overenthusiastic, so much so that her words convinced the queen that the opposite of what the person claimed was true.

People in postbiblical times redefined *kedusha* as "holiness" and applied the attribute "holy" to men, women, and articles that they thought were important, once they realized that others did not think so. No one thought of describing Abraham, Isaac, Jacob, Moses, Sarah, Rebecca, and others as "holy" because everyone agreed that these ancient figures were good and significant people. However, kabbalists did name Isaac Luria, the sixteenth-century mystic, *ha'Ari hakadosh*, "the holy Ari," because rational thinkers criticized as unreasonable the Ari's view of God being made up of ten parts, which became separated and required people's help to be reassembled. They referred to the thirteenth-century mystical book Zohar as the *Zohar hakadosh*, "the holy Zohar," because while *zohar* means enlightenment, nonmystics thought its ideas, like those of the Ari, were bizarre and irrational.

Similarly, they called the biblical Joseph, Jacob's son, *Yosef hatzadik*, "righteous Joseph," because there were people who disagreed with their assessment that Joseph always acted properly, and felt that Joseph had behaved improperly when he failed to visit his father for some twenty years while he, Joseph, was a power in Egypt. He also tricked his brothers when they traveled to Egypt seeking food during a famine. Some rabbis in Midrashim even claimed that while Joseph was enslaved in Egypt before his elevation, he entered his master's suite to seduce his master's wife, and only rushed out frightened when he had a vision of his absent father shouting, "This is wrong!"[2]

Even today, many Chasidim and non-Jewish mystics call their clerics "holy" because they are "protesting" that the religious teacher's lessons are correct and that they are doing what is right when they accept the cleric's teaching.

CEREMONIES

"Holiness" also does not exist in the beautiful Jewish ceremonies. The Shabbat does not add one whit of holiness to the day. The Shabbat ceremonies are only reminders to treat the Sabbath day differently and take the actions that are taught by the Shabbat. It is the actions that one learns from the Shabbat that is crucial.[3]

---

2. Babylonian Talmud, *Sota* 36b.

3. The marriage ceremony is called *kiddushin* in Hebrew and the Sabbath begins with the *kiddush*

Needless to say, not everyone agreed that the definition of *kedusha* is separation.

THE VIEW OF SAMUEL DAVID LUZZATTO

Luzzatto recognized that holiness added nothing to an object or person, but wrote that *kodesh* was derived from *kad esh*, "a burning of fire," and the term originally applied to sacrifices that were burned in order to honor God.[4] Later, the term was transferred to anything that was set aside for God's honor and separated from profane use, even when no burning was involved. A person could be called holy if the person was devoted to God and separated for divine service. Thus, Luzzatto's view is similar to the generally accepted scholarly view, but Nachmanides accepted the ubiquitous meaning.

NACHMANIDES AND ISRAEL

Nachmanides contended that the land of Israel is "holy," using the current understanding of the term, and developed mystical ideas. Nachmanides had a profound love of the land of Israel, which he considered sacred ground, and he insisted that settlement in Israel was a divine commandment.[5] His feeling that Israel was holy was so intense that he stated that God killed Jacob's beloved second wife Rachel just prior to the family entering the land of Israel so that the patriarch Jacob, who was allowed to marry two sisters outside of Israel, would not violate the Torah's command forbidding matrimony with two sisters in Israel, thereby desecrating the holy earth.[6]

---

made over wine. Both Hebrew words are derived from a root which is translated today as "holiness." Yet, contrary to what many believe, neither the ceremony of marriage nor the one that introduces the Sabbath produce holiness. The words are used in connection with marriage and the Sabbath to teach that they *can be significant if they are properly observed.*

4. Commentary to Exodus 15:11.

5. *Sefer Hamitzvot l'Harambam im Hasagot Haramban*, ed. Charles Ber Chavel (Jerusalem: Mossad Harav Kook, 1981).

6. Nachmanides maintained that the patriarchs learned the Torah by divine inspiration and observed it centuries before the Torah was revealed during the days of Moses. He also contended that the observance of the Torah commands applies only in the land of Israel (commentary to Genesis 26:5 and Leviticus 18:25). See Joseph Bonfils, *Tzaphnat Paneiach*, ed. D. Herzog (Heidelberg, 1930), volume 2; and Hasdai ibn Shaprut, *Tzaphnat Paneiach* (same title as Bonfils), Ms. Oxford-Bodley Opp. Add. 40–107 (Neubauer 2350), beginning on 53b.

Nachmanides was convinced that God only exercises divine power in Israel, for only Israel is a holy land. God set other divine-like powers to control other lands. "There is in this matter a secret relating to that which the rabbis have said [in the above quoted Talmudic statement]: 'He who dwells outside of the land of Israel is like one who has no God.'"[7] Nachmanides understood the Talmud to mean that people who live outside of Israel are under the influence and power of these other supernatural beings; even if they try to worship God, it is as if they have no God.

This love of the land of Israel also led Nachmanides to the doctrine that all the Torah commandments are only divinely obligated upon those who are dwelling in Israel. Outside of the land, Jews observe the laws only so that they will not be "new to us" when we return to the land of Israel.[8]

HOLINESS AND PROPHECY

There are essentially two understandings of prophecy. The most widespread notion, articulated by the poet Judah Halevi in his book *The Kuzari* and by many others, is that a prophet is a "holy" man, and with rare exceptions a "holy" woman, who lives a life of remarkable piety. This individual must, except for extremely rare occasions (Balaam being virtually a sole example), be Jewish. God selects this person in order to communicate something to Jews (Jonah prophesying to Nineveh is an exception). Prophecy only occurs in Israel because the land is "holy" and the "holiness" of prophecy would be inappropriate elsewhere. The prophet says only what God tells him to say. Whatever he says, therefore, is true. However, God can change the decree that the prophet announces under certain circumstances, such as when people change their behavior – as they did when Jonah told the people of Nineveh that they would perish, but they changed their ways and were saved.

MAIMONIDES

Maimonides held a contrary view.[9] Maimonides felt that objects could not be holy;

---

7. *Ramban: Commentary on the Torah*, trans. and annotated Charles Ber Chavel, vol. 1, *Genesis* (New York: Shilo, 1971), 359, commentary to Genesis 28:21.

8. See his commentary to Leviticus 18:25 and Deuteronomy 11:18 and his *Sermon on the Words of Kohelet*.

9. Nachmanides did not agree with the listing of the 613 commandments that Maimonides placed in his *Sefer Hamitzvot*. One disagreement was that Maimonides did not include dwelling

that would be unnatural. He recognized Israel's historical importance to the Jewish people, and he personally had great fondness for the land, but he did not think that it was holy or that it radiated a supernatural element that improved one's life.

When he was escaping from the fanatical Muslims in Spain and Morocco, Maimonides and his family went to Israel, wanting to settle there in peace. However, when he saw that virtually all of the Jewish inhabitants of the land were impoverished physically and intellectually, he and his family decided instead to continue their journey and settle in Egypt, where he remained for the rest of his life. He ultimately became the Nagid, the religious and political leader, of the Egyptian Jewish community, and his descendants held this position for several generations after his death.

SUMMARY

Is the Bible "holy"? No. The Bible does not make this claim. *Kedusha* means "separate." We need to live a life that separates ourselves from all that is harmful. If we obey biblical teachings, Maimonides tells us that we can learn some truths, improve ourselves, and help others and society improve as well.

---

in Israel as a command, while Nachmanides insisted that it was a biblical command. See *Sefer Hamitzvot l'Harambam im Hasagot Haramban* regarding Nachmanides's views, and Menachem Kellner's *Maimonides' Confrontation with Mysticism* (Littman Library of Jewish Civilization, 2006) about Maimonides's views on holiness.

Repentance – Not a Biblical Concept

Parts of Hosea 14, beginning with 14:2, are read as the haphtarah two or three times a year – with the portion of Vayeitzei, on Shabbat Shuva (the Shabbat between Rosh Hashanah and Yom Kippur), and sometimes with the portion Vayeilekh. This practice is based on the idea that a person can return to God by doing teshuva, *repentance – an idea that the rabbis felt the prophet Hosea was teaching when he wrote "Shuva Yisrael ad Hashem elokekha," "Return Israel to the Lord your God" (Babylonian Talmud, Yoma 86a). According to the rabbis, repentance is accomplished by pointing out one's misdeeds during prayers to God.*

The rabbis believed that Hosea was a descendant of Jacob's firstborn Reuben, who they say was the first of Jacob's sons to do *teshuva* for selling their brother Joseph. *Genesis Rabba* 84:18–19 states that God said: "'By your life, a descendant of yours will begin and open the gates of repentance.' Who was this? This was Hosea, who said, 'Return, Israel, unto the Lord your God.'"

As I pointed out in the commentary to 14:2, Hosea was not speaking about *teshuva,* and neither Hosea nor any other prophet who lived during his time or before ever mentions repentance.

As I wrote in my book *Mysteries of Judaism:*[1]

Repentance, *teshuva* in Hebrew, is a practical endeavor.[2] Repentance doesn't

---

1. *Mysteries of Judaism* (Jerusalem: Gefen Publishing House, 2014), 8–9.
2. Most people understand repentance and confessions as they do sacrifices, as pseudo-magical recitations that remove misdeeds – as if words recited during a synagogue service could somehow

magically absolve people of wrongs they committed. It's not abracadabra. Jewish repentance practices remind people to take practical measures to correct their mistakes. Maimonides put it this way:[3] *teshuva* is when a person decides to abandon his or her past misdeeds, resolves not to do them again, thinks how to correct them, and develops habits to assure they are not repeated.

Neither the term *teshuva* nor the concept of repentance as we know it today appear in the Torah. The ancients, Israelites and non-Israelites, believed that what one said, especially vows, or what one did cannot be erased. When an egg is broken, its shards cannot be reassembled. Misdeeds, they thought, are remedied only by punishment.[4]

Scholars suppose that the current idea that people can nullify misdeeds by doing *teshuva* developed in three stages.[5] It began around 722 BCE, centuries after King Solomon's death, when his kingdom split into two with Israel in the north and Judea in the south.[6] In that year, the Assyrians conquered Israel and exiled most Israelites from their land.[7] The Judeans who saw the cyclopean catastrophe were convinced that the disaster occurred because of the misdeeds of the northern tribes, especially their abandonment of God and worship of idols.[8] They knew that they had done the same and searched for a way to save themselves, to nullify their wrongs without punishment. It was then that *teshuva* began to develop as an idea that repentance can erase prior misdeeds. It was further entrenched after 586 BCE when Judea itself was destroyed by the Babylonians and many Judeans were exiled to Babylon. The

---

change the past, erase the slap a husband gave his wife, and restore a loving relationship. "I don't understand why you're still angry," the husband wails. "I did *teshuva* in the synagogue!" This isn't the way life works.

3. *Mishneh Torah, Hilkhot Teshuva*.

4. This concept is still reflected in the Talmudic view that death atones. Babylonian Talmud, *Shabbat* 32a, *Yoma* 86a, *Sanhedrin* 43b and 47a–b.

5. Olam Hatanakh, *Devarim* (Keter, 2002), 221–23.

6. Ten tribes in northern Israel and Transjordan revolted and formed their own nation after Solomon's son Rehoboam refused to reduce their taxes.

7. Some escaped to the south, to Judea, but the rest disappeared from history and are known today as "the ten lost tribes."

8. See Hosea 8:5–13. Hosea was an eighth-century BCE prophet in Israel.

final stage began in 70 CE when the second temple was destroyed by Rome, when Jews felt again that their misdeeds caused the destruction and rabbis developed practices that they hoped would rid Jews of wrongs.

Was the Golden Calf an Idol?

During the time of Moses, many Bible commentators argued that while the Israelites worshipped the golden calf, they did not treat the calf as a god, but as a symbol associated with God, similar to a mezuzah.

SCHOLARLY VIEW

The *Encyclopaedia Judaica*[1] summarizes the scholarly view: "The bull had an important role in the art and religious texts of the ancient near East.... Jeroboam's calves corresponded to the cherubim of Solomon's Temple, i.e., they were regarded as seats or pedestals upon which the Lord was thought to stand, invisible to human eyes.... [The] calves were placed in the courts of the temple.... In any event, Jeroboam's initiative must have had some basis in an old tradition, otherwise he could not have succeeded in his enterprise."

EHRLICH

Ehrlich[2] argued that the use of the golden calf was part of the worship service of ancient Israel; it was a symbol of God. He wrote that the story of the golden calf in Exodus chapter 32 must have been composed long after the days of Moses. This explains why none of the prophets who criticized the Israelites' behavior during the desert wanderings mention it. The only reference to it is Psalm 106, which was composed during a much later period. It was only the later prophets who felt that the use of the golden calf was wrong.

---

1. S.v. "Golden Calf."
2. In his commentary to Hosea 12:1, I Kings 12:29, II Kings 10:31, and other places.

Around 922 BCE, Jeroboam I and ten of the twelve tribes broke away from the kingdom of King Rehoboam, grandson of King David. Jeroboam established two new temples in his northern kingdom, in Beth-el and Dan, and placed in them two golden calves, as detailed in I Kings 12:28. Jeroboam told his people, "Behold your God, Israel, who brought you up out of the land of Egypt." Ehrlich states that it makes no sense to think that Jeroboam could have persuaded the people that the calf had brought them out of Egypt if they had not used the golden calves in the past. Therefore, Jeroboam must have been referring to their long-held belief that God is represented by a calf. Thus, even later, when King Jehu destroyed Baal out of Israel, he did not cease using the golden calves in Beth-el and Dan.[3]

RASHI

Rashi had a nonrational view of the golden calf during the days of Moses. He elaborated on a Midrash mentioned in the Babylonian Talmud, *Shabbat* 89a, and in *Exodus Rabba*.[4] He suggested that the Israelites were misled by the demon Satan, who scared the people by creating frightening turmoil in heaven and anxiety-producing darkness. Satan told the people that Moses was dead and proved it by showing them Moses's bier. The non-Israelite mixed multitude who accompanied the Israelites during the exodus were the first to succumb. They in turn enticed some, but not many, Israelites to join them. They threatened Aaron with death. Aaron tried many tricks to delay them from carrying out their plan to substitute a calf for God. However, Satan harried the people. Aaron was assisted by magicians among the people, who produced the golden calf instantly through magic.

---

3. II Kings 10:29.
4. Rashi to Exodus 32.

The Prophet Micah's Ignorance of the Torah

In the other volumes in this series, I show that none of the Israelite leaders and prophets seemed to know about the Torah. There are also suggestions that the ancient Israelites knew nothing about the Torah until probably the time of King Josiah (649–609 BCE).[1]

Among the many examples that could be cited to support the claim that the Israelites did not know of the Torah, it is significant that no biblical book until the time of King Josiah mentions Moses's Torah;[2] no Israelite leader or prophet ever criticizes the people for violating Torah laws, even though they frequently criticize them for their faults; some post-Moses practices are significantly different than those mentioned in Moses's Torah, such as the levirate marriage of Ruth; and there is no indication in the Bible that the Israelites observed important holidays mentioned in the Torah, such as the Sabbath and the Festival of Matzot, which commemorated the exodus from Egyptian slavery. Joshua and the Israelites totally ignored the clear, often-repeated mandate in Numbers 33:50–56 that the Israelites must expel all Canaanites from Canaan lest they be a thorn upon them and entice them to worship idols. The Israelites not only failed to obey this Torah divine command, but there is no indication that they even considered it; it is as if they knew nothing about it. Instead, they allowed the Canaanites to remain in the

---

1. See II Kings 22–23 and II Chronicles 34–35, which tell of the people finding part of the Torah.
2. "Torah" could refer to the Five Books of Moses, the entire Jewish Tanakh, or just a teaching. The Bible does not use it in the prior two forms in the Five Books of Moses and the post-Moses period until the time of King Josiah.

country and took tribute from them, until the Canaanites grew strong, became a thorn upon them, and enticed many to worship idols.[3]

The prophet Micah is another example of a prophet who apparently knew nothing about the Torah. The book of Micah contains seven chapters in which the prophet constantly criticizes both the southern nation of Judah and the northern nation of Israel for improper behavior and promises that they will be destroyed as a consequence of their acts. But despite the catalogue of wrongs, Micah never mentions that they violated the Torah of Moses or failed to observe the Torah's holidays, such as the Sabbath and the three festivals of Passover, Shavuot, and Succoth.

Micah lived at the same time as Amos, Hosea, Jonah, and First Isaiah, around the time of the destruction of the northern kingdom of Israel in 722 BCE. He berates the people for basic immorality: "They covet fields, and seize them; and houses and take them away; they oppress a man and his household in this way, a man and his heritage" (2:2); "You cast out the women of my people from their pleasant houses; you take away my glory forever from their young children" (2:9). Micah castigates his people for lying, robbery, murder, bribery, and violence. He relates that priests and prophets charge for their teachings, merchants use deceitful weights, and people show disrespect to parents and in-laws. In 4:2, he mentions that non-Israelites will ascend the mountain of the Lord and God will teach them the divine ways and laws, but he does not mention the Torah of Moses.[4] In 4:6, he states that the Israelites "will walk in the name of the Lord our God for ever and ever," but he does not say that they will observe the Torah of Moses.

---

3. There is one statement that seemingly contradicts this view. Joshua 22:5 reports Joshua warning the Transjordanian tribes to "heed the commandments and the Torah that Moses the servant of the Lord commanded you, to love the Lord your God, and to walk in his ways, and to keep his commandments, and to cling to him, and to serve him with all your heart and entire being." This could be seen as a refutation of the idea that the Israelites knew nothing about the Torah: it mentions Moses's Torah and the words are similar to those in Deuteronomy 6. However, as previously stated, while the term Torah refers today to the Pentateuch or entire Bible or Jewish teachings, it simply means "teachings" when used in the Bible. Also the wording, while similar, is not exact and may not be a quote. In addition, scholars claim that the book of Deuteronomy was discovered and used during the reign of King Josiah when the book of Joshua was composed, so this language could have been inserted at that time.

4. The word for laws is *torah*, which does not mean the Torah of Moses. And, in context, it could not refer to Moses's Torah since it is speaking about non-Israelites. See previous note.

In 6:4, Micah states that God sent Moses, Aaron, and Miriam to redeem the Israelites from Egyptian slavery, as if he did not know that the Torah states that God sent only Moses.[5] In 6:6–8 he responds to the people, who desire to atone for their transgressions by offering God animal sacrifices, or even their firstborn sons. As in Hosea 6:6, Micah tells his people that God does not want sacrifices but moral behavior, and he does not mention the Torah. "It has been told to you, man, what is good and what the Lord requires of you: only to act justly, and love mercy, and walk humbly with your God."

---

5. The Targum invents a role for each: Moses to teach religion and law, Aaron to teach how to repent, and Miriam to give instruction to women.

Afterword

The Babylonian Talmud, Bava Batra 14b, states that the writings of twelve prophets were placed together in a single book called Trei Asar, *"Twelve," to preserve them, since small individual books might be lost.[1] Hosea was placed first either because it was one of the largest books or because the Talmudic rabbis felt that Hosea was the first of the twelve prophets.[2] Hosea prophesied during and after the reign of Jeroboam II in the northern kingdom called Israel.[3] Four other prophets prophesied at the same time, but none mentions the others.[4] They were Amos, Micah, Isaiah, and Jonah of II Kings 14.[5] The Talmud contends that Hosea was a greater prophet than his contemporaries, including Isaiah.[6] The Talmudic rabbis state that Hosea developed the idea of repentance. They felt that repentance is extremely important in daily life, and particularly during the Ten Days of Penitence that they established between Rosh Hashanah and Yom Kippur.*

---

1. This explanation cannot be entirely true because the book of Ruth, for example, is also small, consisting of only four chapters. But perhaps Ruth was kept separate because it was considered special by the Jewish community.
2. Some scholars insist that Amos preceded him.
3. It is unclear exactly when Jeroboam II reigned. William F. Albright in *The Mysterious Numbers of the Hebrew Kings*, Eerdmans, 1965, suggests a forty-one-year reign from 786 to 746 BCE.
4. This is very strange since all five men prophesied at the same time. What does this say about their prophecies? Does it tell us that they made no impression at the time?
5. Curiously, the Talmud, rabbis, and scholars fail to mention Jonah as one of the prophets who lived at the time of Jeroboam II even though II Kings 14 explicitly states that he gave advice from God to the king.
6. *Pesachim* 87a. The Talmud compares Isaiah to Moses, so this is huge praise.

THE BOOK OF HOSEA

- The Talmud states: "The Men of the Great Assembly wrote Ezekiel, the Twelve Minor Prophets, Daniel, and the Scroll of Esther."[7] Thus, according to the Talmud, the book of Hosea was composed centuries after the prophet's death. Jews felt that the message of the book was so significant that portions from the book are read after the Shabbat Torah reading as the haphtarah on four different weeks.
- The book of Hosea contains 197 verses in fourteen chapters. The verses are filled with dramatic metaphors. Virtually all of the 197 verses are obscure and subject to various, often contradictory interpretations. The overall mood of the book is one of disappointment and betrayal. Hosea beseeches his people, the nation of Israel, to return to God. He berates them with nonstop criticism. The prophet reveals nothing about himself in his book, with the possible exception being in a failed marriage to a woman who deserted him and engaged in adulterous sex. However, this story may be a parable dramatizing the Israelites' desertion of God.
- We do not know if Hosea's wife left him to become a temple prostitute, a street whore, or an adulteress with one or more men. We also do not know if any of her children resulted from such unions.

THE BOOK'S MESSAGE

- Hosea likens the Israelites' behavior to desertion, but the exact nature of their sin is obscure. The general consensus is that the nation abandoned God and worshipped idols.[8] However, it is possible to interpret verses as saying that the

---

7. *Bava Batra* 15a. Translation from *The Babylonian Talmud, Seder Nezikin*, vol. 2. This raises several problems: Does "wrote" mean that the Men of the Great Assembly composed the book from fresh or that they edited material that they had received from previous generations? If they wrote it anew, where did they get Hosea's prophecies? If they edited material, what texts did they have, and did they add and remove language from what they had? Additionally, who were the Men of the Great Assembly? Scholars admit that they do not know, but imagine this was a council established by Ezra the Scribe to aid him in writing and editing the Torah texts. See Hoenig, *The Great Sanhedrin*. Ezra came to Israel in around 433 BCE, some three hundred years after the death of Jeroboam II. See *The Jewish Encyclopedia* (Ktav, 1901).
8. This view seems to be supported by 2:10, where Baal can refer to the practice of non-Israelites. Further support may be found in 2:15, 18, and 19, and 3:1, where Baal and "other gods" could be understood as describing Gomer's leaving Hosea to serve as a temple prostitute. In addition,

nation of Israel was worshipping God, not idols, in their temples, and Hosea was berating them because God does not want sacrifices, but proper treatment of fellow citizens. This seems to be the meaning of verse 6:6, where Hosea criticizes the people of Israel for thinking that their sacrifices to God satisfy the deity: "For I desire mercy, not sacrifice, and knowledge of God rather than burnt offerings." Support for this idea is found in 8:1 and 9:8, where Hosea calls the temple in Beth-el "the house of the Lord"; in 8:13, where he says, "They offer sacrifices of fire to me, let them sacrifice and eat the meat, which the Lord does not accept."

THE BOOK'S CONTENT

- Most of Hosea's comments are critical; he gives examples of wrongs committed by people in a hyperbolic manner with no example of a person doing what is right. This raises questions about his personality: Is he generally a pessimistic person? His comments are frequently disjointed, and move from one subject to another and then back again after just a few verses. We do not know if this reflects his rambling thinking, or if it is the fault of the editor of his book. He also repeats ideas frequently.[9]
- Some scholars note that from time to time Hosea criticizes Judah. They insist that these statements were added by the writers (or editors) in Judah because Hosea only addressed his own nation Israel.

THE BOOK'S IMPORTANCE

- Jews have considered the book important: (1) The Talmud states that Hosea was more important than Isaiah, and the Talmud compares Isaiah to Moses.[10] (2) Chapters of the book are read as the haphtarah after the Torah readings in synagogues on four occasions, including on the Shabbat between Rosh Hashanah and Yom Kippur. This is close to 10 percent of the times that haphtarahs are read. Chapter 14 is read twice during the year.

---

while the following verses are not explicitly referring to idol worship, it is possible to argue that they are berating Israel for idol worship: 4:14, 4:17, 5:3, and 8:5–6.

9. This is the comment of my study partners Dr. and Mrs. Norman and Estelle Wald. Some modern critiques blame this on the editors.

10. *Pesachim* 87a.

- While the book contains many rebukes of the people, it also contains many statements emphasizing God's love of Israel.
- The message to act properly with others is a significant lesson. All too many people still think that as long as they pray and read the Torah and Talmud they are doing what God desires, even while they act immorally.
- Two verses from Hosea expressing God's love of Israel are read daily by men when they put on the *tefillin* before the morning service.[11] The *tefillin* reminds Jews to obey God's commands.

PROBLEMS PRESENTED BY THE BOOK

- One of the most perplexing issues in the book is whether Hosea knew about the Five Books of Moses. It could be argued that he did not. Although he rebukes his people frequently for their bad behavior, in chapter 4 he lists ten ways that the Israelites violate God's will, and even mentions some prohibitions that are in the Decalogue (Ten Commandments), yet he never mentions that they violated the Torah or the Decalogue. He also does not speak about the Sabbath and holidays, with the possible exception of Succoth, nor does he refer to the golden calf or the desert murmurings.
- If 2:4 is understood to mean that Hosea divorced his wife who then married another, and divorced this second man, Hosea violates Deuteronomy 24:1–4.
- Verse 3:4 indicates that Israel used sacred pillars and seems to condone the practice even though this violates Deuteronomy 16:22.
- Additionally, in 11:8 Admah and Zeboim are cited, but not Sodom and Gomorrah, the two cities mentioned as being destroyed in Genesis 14. This may indicate that Hosea may not have had the book of Genesis and relied on a tradition that differed from it.
- In a similar vein, Hosea's reference to Jacob's wrestling against an adversary contrasts significantly with the account in Genesis 32:25. While Genesis does not disclose the identity of Jacob's wrestler, Hosea states that his assailant was an angel. The prophet also includes additional details that are not stated in Genesis. Most significantly, Hosea states that the episode occurred in Beth-el, whereas Genesis places it in Wadi Jabbok.

---

11. 2:30–31.

- Hosea seems to be consistent with the books of Joshua, Judges, Samuel, and other books of the Bible, according to which the people at that time seemed to know nothing about the Torah.
- Verse 9:4 may be allowing the offering of sacrifices to God in foreign lands, which the rabbis say is prohibited.
- Verse 9:9 may be saying that God punishes children for the misdeeds of their parents.
- Verse 12:5, which states that God will speak with Israel in Beth-el, may confirm that the temple in Beth-el was dedicated to God and was not a site of idol worship, and may support the view that Hosea felt that God intended the area of Shiloh and Beth-el as the capital of the nation and its spiritual center.
- Also, the prophet does not mention Amos, Micah, Isaiah, and Jonah who also prophesied at the same time. Did he not know of their existence? Or did the writers (or editors) of the book not know that they prophesied at the same time?

References

Albright, William Foxwell. *The Mysterious Numbers of the Hebrew Kings*. Eerdmans, 1965.

Andersen, Francis I., and David Noel Freedman. *Hosea*. Anchor Yale Bible Commentaries. New York: Doubleday, 1996.

Babylonian Talmud: *Avoda Zara, Bava Batra, Berakhot, Kiddushin, Megillah, Pesachim, Sanhedrin, Shabbat, Yevamot, Yoma.*

Bonfils, Joseph. *Tzaphnat Paneiach*. Edited by D. Herzog. Heidelberg, 1930.

Buttrick, George A., ed. *Lamentations, Ezekiel, Daniel, Twelve Prophets*. Vol. 6 of the Interpreter's Bible. New York: Abingdon, 1957.

Cathcart, Kevin J., and Robert P. Gordon. *The Targum of the Minor Prophets*. Wilmington, DE: Michael Glazier, 1989.

Crescas, Hasdai. *The Refutation of the Christian Principles*. SUNY Series in Jewish Philosophy. New York: State University of New York Press, 1992.

Drazin, Israel. *Mysteries of Judaism*. Jerusalem: Gefen Publishing House, 2014.

———. *Ruth, Esther, and Judith*. Unusual Bible Interpretations. Jerusalem: Gefen Publishing House, 2016.

———. *Jonah and Amos*. Unusual Bible Interpretations. Jerusalem: Gefen Publishing House, 2016.

———. *Joshua*. Unusual Bible Interpretations. Jerusalem: Gefen Publishing House, 2014.

———. *Judges*. Unusual Bible Interpretations. Jerusalem: Gefen Publishing House, 2015.

Driver, G. R. "Studies in the Vocabulary of the Old Testament, VIII." *Journal of Theological Studies* 36 (1935): 293–301.

Ehrlich, Arnold Bogumil. *Mikra Kipheshuto*. Edited by Harry M. Orlinsky. New York: Ktav, 1969.

Encyclopaedia Judaica. Jerusalem: Keter, 1971–1972.

Epstein, Isidore, ed. *The Babylonian Talmud*. Soncino, 1935.

Halevi, Judah. *Sefer Hakuzari*.

Harper, William Rainey. *A Critical and Exegetical Commentary on Amos and Hosea*. International Critical Commentary. Charles Scribner's Sons, 1905.

Hoenig, Sidney B. *The Great Sanhedrin*. Philadelphia: Dropsie College, 1953.

ibn Shaprut, Hasdai. *Tzaphnat Paneiach*. Ms. Oxford-Bodley Opp. Add. 40–107, Neubauer 2350.

Jewish Publication Society. *The Holy Scriptures*. Jewish Publication Society, 1960.

Josephus. *Antiquities*.

———. *Wars of the Jews*.

Kellner, Menachem. *Maimonides' Confrontation with Mysticism*. Littman Library of Jewish Civilization, 2006.

Kil, Yehuda. Commentary to Hosea. In *Trei Asar*, vol. 1. Daat Mikra. Jerusalem: Mossad Harav Kook, 1973.

Ktav. *The Jewish Encyclopedia*. Ktav, 1901.

Lehrman, S. M. "Introduction and Commentary." In *The Twelve Prophets: Hebrew Text, English Translation and Commentary*. Edited by Abraham Cohen. Soncino, 1957.

Luzzatto, Samuel David. *Peirush al Chamisha Chumshei Torah*. Tel Aviv: Dvir, 1971.

Maimonides, Moses (Rambam). *Guide of the Perplexed*. Edited by M. Friedlander. New York: Dover, 1881.

———. *Mishneh Torah*.

———. *Peirush Hamishna*.

———. *Sefer Hamitzvot l'Harambam im Hasagot Haramban*. Edited by Charles Ber Chavel. Jerusalem: Mossad Harav Kook, 1981.

———. *Shemonah Perakim: Introduction to Ethics of the Fathers*. Edited by J. J. Garfinkel. New York: 1912.

McKeating, Henry. *Amos, Hosea, Micah*. Cambridge Bible Commentary. Cambridge University Press, 1971.

Midrashim: *Exodus Rabba, Genesis Rabba, Leviticus Rabba, Pirkei d'Rabbi Eliezer, Sifrei, Tanchuma, Yalkut Shimoni*.

Mishnayot: *Sota.*

Nachmanides. *Ramban: Commentary on the Torah.* Translated and annotated by
    Charles Ber Chavel. Vol. 1, *Genesis.* New York: Shilo, 1971.

———. *Sefer Hamitzvot l'Harambam im Hasagot Haramban.* Edited by Charles
    Ber Chavel. Jerusalem: Mossad Harav Kook, 1981.

———. "Sermon on the Words of Kohelet." In *Kitvei Ramban,* vol. 1, edited by
    Charles Ber Chavel. Jerusalem: Mossad Harav Kook, 1963.

Nyberg, H. S. *Studien zum Hosea Buch.* Uppsala: Lundequistaka, 1935.

Revised Standard Version of the Bible. National Council of the Churches of Christ
    in the USA, 1946–2006.

Scriptures and Apocrypha sources (Pentateuch/Prophets/Writings): Amos,
    I Chronicles, Ezekiel, Hosea, Isaiah, Jeremiah, Job, Joel, John, Jonah,
    Joshua, Judges, Judith, I/II Kings, Malachi, Micah, Philippians, Pentateuch,
    Peshitta, Paul, Psalms, Proverbs, Ruth, I/II Samuel, Septuagint, Song of
    Songs, Trypho.

Segal, M. T. *Hoshea.* Olam Hatanakh. Divrei Hayamim, 2002.

Smolar, Leivy, and Moses Aberbach. *Studies in Targum Jonathan to the Prophets.*
    New York: Ktav, 1983.

Index

About the Author

DR. ISRAEL DRAZIN

EDUCATION: Dr. Drazin, born in 1935, received three rabbinical degrees in 1957, a BA in theology in 1957, an MEd in psychology in 1966, a JD in law in 1974, an MA in Hebrew literature in 1978, and a PhD with honors in Aramaic literature in 1981. Thereafter, he completed two years of postgraduate study in both philosophy and mysticism and graduated the US Army's Command and General Staff College and its War College for generals in 1985.

MILITARY: Brigadier General Drazin entered army active duty at age twenty-one, as the youngest US chaplain ever to serve on active duty. He served on active duty from 1957 to 1960 in Louisiana and Germany, and then joined the active reserves and soldiered, in increasing grades, with half a dozen units. From 1978 until 1981, he lectured at the US Army Chaplains School on legal subjects. In March 1981, the army requested that he take leave from civil service and return to active duty to handle special constitutional issues. He was responsible for preparing the defense in the trial challenging the constitutionality of the army chaplaincy; the military chaplaincies of all the uniformed services, active and reserve, as well as the Veteran's Administration, were attacked utilizing a constitutional rationale and could have been disbanded. The government won the action in 1984, and Drazin was awarded the prestigious Legion of Merit. Drazin returned to civilian life and the active reserves in 1984 as assistant chief of chaplains, the highest reserve officer position available in the army chaplaincy, with the rank of brigadier general. He was the first Jewish person to serve in this capacity in the US Army. During his military career, he revolutionized the role of military chaplains, making them officers responsible for the free exercise rights of all military personnel and requiring them to provide for the needs of people of all faiths as well as atheists. General Drazin completed this four-year tour of duty with honors in March 1988, culminating a total of thirty-one years of military duty.

ATTORNEY: Israel Drazin graduated from law school in 1974 and immediately began a private practice. He handled virtually all manners of suits, including domestic, criminal, bankruptcy, accident, and contract cases. He joined with his son in 1993 and formed offices in Columbia and Dundalk, Maryland. Dr. Drazin stopped actively practicing law in 1997, after twenty-three years, and became "Of Counsel" to the law offices of Drazin and Drazin, PA.

CIVIL SERVICE: Israel Drazin joined the US Civil Service in 1962 and remained a civil service employee, with occasional leave for military duty, until retirement in 1990. At retirement he had accumulated thirty-one years of creditable service. During his US Civil Service career, he held many positions including being an equal opportunity consultant in the 1960s (advising insurance company top executives regarding civil rights and equal employment) and the head of Medicare's Civil Litigation Staff (supervising a team of lawyers who handled suits filed by and against the government's Medicare program). He also served as the director for all Maryland's federal agencies' relationships with the United Fund.

RABBI: Dr. Drazin was ordained as a rabbi in 1957 at Ner Israel Rabbinical College in Baltimore, Maryland, and subsequently received *semichot* from two other rabbis. He entered army active duty in 1957. He left active duty in 1960 and officiated as a weekend rabbi at several synagogues, including being the first rabbi in Columbia, Maryland. He continued the uninterrupted weekend rabbinical practice until 1974 and then officiated as a rabbi on an intermittent basis until 1987. His rabbinical career totaled thirty years.

PHILANTHROPY: Dr. Drazin served as the executive director of the Jim Joseph Foundation, a charitable foundation that gives money to support Jewish education, for just over four years, from September 2000 to November 2004.

AUTHOR: Israel Drazin is the author of thirty-five books, more than three hundred popular and scholarly articles, and over thirty-five hundred book and movie reviews. In addition to editing a book on legends, he has written a book about the case he handled for the US army, children's books, and numerous scholarly books on the philosopher Maimonides and on the Aramaic translation of the Bible. His website is www.booksnthoughts.com.

MEMBERSHIPS AND AWARDS: Brigadier General Drazin is admitted to practice law in Maryland, the Federal Court, and before the US Supreme Court. He is a member of several attorney bar associations and the Rabbinical Council of America (RCA). He was honored with a number of military awards, the RCA 1985 Joseph Hoenig Memorial Award, and the Jewish Welfare Board 1986 Distinguished Service Award. Mayor Kurt Schmoke, of Baltimore, Maryland, named February 8, 1988 "Israel Drazin Day." A leading Baltimore Synagogue named him "Man of the Year" in 1990. He is included in recent editions of *Who's Who in World Jewry*, *Who's Who in American Law*, *Who's Who in Biblical Studies and Archaeology*, and other *Who's Who* volumes.